BEAGLE TALES 6

BY
BOB FORD

SUNBURY
P R E S S

Mechanicsburg, Pennsylvania USA

Published by Sunbury Press, Inc.
Mechanicsburg, Pennsylvania

www.sunburypress.com

ISBN: 978-1-62006-792-5 (Trade Paperback)
ISBN: 978-1-62006-793-2 (Mobipocket)

Library of Congress Control Number: 2017934256

FIRST SUNBURY PRESS EDITION: March 2017

Product of the United States of America
0 1 1 2 3 5 8 13 21 34 55

Set in Bookman Old Style
Designed by Lawrence Knorr
Cover by Lawrence Knorr
Cover Photo by Bob Ford
Edited by Allyson Gard

Continue the Enlightenment!

WINTER DAYS

When I was a kid, there were a few January rituals that characterized most of my time. One of them was Christmas trees. Our beagle club had a running pen, and the road into the enclosure's parking lot was plowed. People would dump Christmas trees there. I now hear all sorts of debate about the value of used Christmas trees in an overall effort to maintain a quality running grounds, as the trees are dead and will shed their needles in time, yielding Christmas tree skeletons, which are not ideal cover. Our club liked them in the winter, and the task at hand became distributing the trees over the running grounds into clumps of decent cover capable of allowing a bunny to hide from air predators.

"How old are you?" the club president asked me.

"I will be 14 soon," I answered.

"How would you like to disperse Christmas trees around the club?" He scratched his chin.

"Where are they?" I asked.

"In the parking lot," he scratched his head. "Space them out. Make piles that are as big as a picnic table. Don't put them on the paths, but put them in places off the feed strips that will grow again in the spring. I don't want to be mowing Christmas trees. Stack them where the cover looks sparse. I will make sure you get a little money for your efforts."

Now early January was still hunting season, so Saturdays were out. That left Sundays to work on this project, as Pennsylvania has never permitted Sunday hunting. I had a paper route that I had to do on Sunday mornings, but I could do this tree job in the afternoon.

"Dad, what are you doing this Sunday?" I asked.

"Working," he said.

"How about the following Sunday?"

"Working." Dad was serious about work, and his job did not give him many Sundays off. Once in a while the work rotation aligned with a calendar that matched up with family events. The factory where he worked did not have a work schedule that was concerned with family events. They had developed a complicated scheme that involved workers changing shifts every week while also varying the days of the week wherein an employee was scheduled to be off. This then was modified by offerings of overtime and a desire to maximize productivity.

"Your mom can drop you off," Dad said. As you can tell, I was going to be left alone to do this work. There would be no adult supervision. This is a great joy that I think kids today are missing, as they have 4P—Perpetual Precautionary Parental Presence. These youngsters cannot even make an embarrassing mistake without their mom taking a video of it on her cell phone and uploading it to social media.

Just recently some friends of mine attended an elementary school play at 1 p.m. on a weekday. In my mind it seems that few parents could attend a play at such an odd time, but they showed up in droves. My father had almost no contact with the school when I was a kid, and if he did it was bad news. Some teachers would try to beat confessions out of mischievous kids back then, as paddling was par for the course. But other disciplinarians utilized far more cruel methods, "Do you want me to call your father at work?" I was asked one time as a lead suspect in a crime ring that involved missing paper and spit balls being directed at other students.

"No! Please don't call my dad at work!" I sobbed, bottom lip quivering. "I did it. I did it. Punish me, please." The sad thing is that I really was innocent, but the last thing I wanted was for my dad to get involved in the investigation. I could hear him saying, "I don't care if you didn't shoot the paper spit balls! You were dumb enough to sit next to kids that did. You should have picked smarter friends. So you are at fault here." Then I would have been forbidden to do something I liked.

Sorry for that digression. As I mentioned the club's access road and the parking lot was plowed. The rest of the club was knee-high snow.

2

"That thing better not poop in my trunk!" my mother grumped as she slid her Buick off the hardtop road and onto the narrow club road that led to the running grounds. Did I mention that January was also a time that I did a lot of box trapping to get rabbits for the club? I had box traps in all my neighbors' yards. This was back when everyone had a garden and no one bought vegetables until late fall or winter at the earliest. Sometimes no vegetables were purchased if the garden had a good year and the canning shelves were packed with produce. I remember one winter that we ate stewed tomatoes as a side dish three times per week and tomato soup every Saturday. It had been a good tomato summer.

Anyway, I assured Mom that even if the rabbit relieved itself, the turds could not get out of the home made, wooden box trap and onto the floor of her trunk. I also explained that rabbits would often eat their own poop the first time it emerged in order to maximize the amount of nutrition that they would get from the vegetation, an amazing adaptation that rabbits had developed in order to survive. Come to think of it, Mom never ate much rabbit after that day even though she would cook it. We pulled into the club parking lot and the sight that lay before us could best be described as what appeared to be a vacant lot that was filled to capacity with cut Christmas trees that were for sale the day after Thanksgiving. And the vendor didn't sell any trees at all. Then they fell over and got snowed upon. Oh, and the needles fell as the wind scattered them (and tinsel) throughout the lot.

"I will be back to get you at dark," Mom said as I was staring in utter disbelief at how many trees were there, "And if I am a little late don't worry. I have to take down our Christmas decorations today." I removed the box trap from the trunk, and Mom sped away. You could never leave a 14 year old in the winter woods without a means of communication today. There would be serious repercussions. I was at a field trial last year, and a guy was glued to his cell phone texting his son, who was at his first rock concert. The dad kept getting pictures of the stage, the performance, and other details of the event. I wondered how the kid could enjoy the concert while taking so many pictures. The father, in turn, was typing sage advice on ways to avoid trouble and stay safe. The dad also sent the kid information that enabled him to buy some souvenirs using Dad's money in PayPal.

My father had given me advice the night before I was scheduled to go drag Christmas trees, briefly speaking to me at bedtime, "Take your coat off when you start working or you might get sweaty and cold. If you get hot and sweaty, don't sit still. Cold can kill ya if you do that. Good night," he waved his hand as I walked upstairs to bed.

I had managed to get ¼ of the trees distributed that day, as I decided to start at the farthest ends of the club first, just in case we got more snow and thus more difficult to walk. Mom wasn't late, which was good. I was so worried about getting sweaty in the cold air that I had removed my coat and my sweatshirt. I started wearing both of them about an hour before she arrived just so I could get warm. We repeated this event for two more Sundays, and I was able to move more trees each week as I was not dragging them as far. I was completely alone with my thoughts for those three days. It was wonderful. I had time to learn how to read tracks in the snow and was amazed at the abundance of songbirds in our running grounds. I contemplated my future plans and managed to get some productive work done at the same time.

As I mentioned earlier, catching rabbits was another January pastime, and it was always welcomed by the neighbors. I would check the "trap line" every day after school and had a plastic toboggan sled to drag the full traps home with me. I would then take the bunnies to the club after supper with my father if he was home at that time, or Mom would reluctantly allow me to put the traps on top of a garbage bag in the trunk of her car and drive me to the beagle club in the event that he was working.

Back then, rabbit season ended in early January. I spent the rest of the month wandering the hills looking for rabbit tracks in the snow so that we had an idea where to hunt the following year. It would be a few years before I bought "Gore Tex" boots that were waterproof. So I used the same thing that everybody else did to keep my feet dry —I put my feet in bread bags before putting them into the boots. You may wonder how well the *Wonder Bread* bag allowed perspiration to leave my feet. The answer to that inquiry is a complex one, but the short answer is that it did not do so very well. But your feet remained merely clammy as opposed to totally soaked, which could happen if you crossed a creek. These January rambles have always been the best method of finding new places for me to hunt rabbits. Any place that still holds bunnies after the snow has toppled the weaker vegetation will certainly have an abundance of chases in the fall.

January is upon us, and we tend to make all sorts of resolutions that we never keep. Perhaps I will resolve to stay a little more disconnected from people. Oh, I don't want to become a hermit or anything. But I would like to walk some strange hills and look for new rabbit cover. Maybe leave that blasted cell phone at home, or at least turn it off. The dad that I mentioned earlier was experiencing the rock concert almost as much as the kid. One was experiencing the concert even whilst filming and the other while watching said video. With the abundance of television shows devoted to hunting and the rise of social media as the primary means of conveying our own stories about the outdoors, I think I will resolve to more fully experience the important places. The running grounds I described earlier are no longer in existence. A little plant has been placed there to compress natural gas so that it can be transmitted in gas lines. I know other places that are now parking lots or housing developments with an intricate maze of cal-de-sacs. I like to think that pictures and videos are a lesser experience than actually being there. For the sake of nostalgia I plan to be alone a little more often. I will start in January, as all resolutions should. It is time I walk a few more hills and find a few more spots to replace the ones that are now covered in concrete or condominiums. But I am not returning to bread bags on my feet.

Maintenance

"Brrr," my wife said as we got into her vehicle to go do some shopping in the advance of a bit of bad weather. We weren't getting milk and bread, don't worry. Ever notice that people who stock up on milk and bread before a big snow also buy a lot of toilet paper? I think that your choice in survival food should be reevaluated if you have to buy 24 rolls of toilet paper to go with it. We usually get groceries for a feast and hope we get stuck at home. If the power goes out I have charcoal to cook on the grill in the snow storm.

"We should be in your truck!" she said, "but you have rendered it incapable of work!"

"It is a hunting truck," I said. Clearly she was talking about the fact that the bed of my truck was consumed with a dog box and a storage bin for carrying tie out stakes, hammers, bowls, and all the other things you need when running dogs. "You will feel better when your car warms up." The car emitted a rapid succession of BEEP BEEP BEEP!

"Yeah," she said, "it should be warm by the time I get to the gas station."

"Was that noise your low fuel light?" I said.

"Yes. Do you mind pumping gas?"

"Not at all," I said, "I wore a coat that is appropriate for the current weather rather than one that had the color that matched the rest of my clothes."

"Thank you!" she beamed, her hair blowing in the full force of the heater vent, which was pointed at her face as she leaned in very close to the dashboard. "I don't like standing at the pump when the tank is this low. It takes too long."

"When do you usually fill the tank?" I asked.

"Usually when that light comes on!" she shouted, as if my head were also so close to the heater as to disrupt hearing.

"Well, what is the size of your gas tank?" I tried to surmise how long it took to fill it.

"I don't know," she parked at the self-serve pump. "Whatever the pump says when you are done. That is the volume of the tank. Because I am about out. That light came on yesterday too."

As you can see, she knows nothing about her car. Or nearly nothing. I dread driving the thing. There is no real way to know what will happen when you start the engine. The wiper blades may be on full force, the radio could be cranked to full volume. It can be terrifying if you aren't properly braced and prepared.

I sometimes feel that way about dogs. I would like to know more about what makes them tick. Years ago I decided to try and do more for my beagles' health and performance, and over time I have made changes. What I am about to say comes from information that I have heard others provide and I won't pretend to be a veterinarian or a canine nutritional specialist. These are all things that have worked for me. I feel like I used to just drive the car, and now I know how to do more—like putting gas into the tank before it is nearly empty and preventing condensation from allowing water to enter the fuel system. Hobbies and habits come in all forms. Feeding a small pack of dogs is one thing, and owning a kennel of 40 dogs is another. I realize that not everything I am saying will be practical, but at the same time, I have seen results.

Dog food is important. I feed *Purina Proplan*, but I know that there are other good foods out there. It is a high protein dog food, and builds muscle mass and endurance. It also is higher in fat, providing energy. I have experienced longevity with my hounds using *Purina*, and that is why I value their product. You will often hear people say that high protein, which helps a dog build muscle mass, will cause kidney failure. This was taught to veterinarians decades ago. I asked my vet about the matter and she told me that high protein is bad for a dog that has kidney failure and can make it worse, but it IS NOT the cause. Kidney failure happens to some old dogs, but the role of protein is not causal. Lion Country Supply held a hunting dog event at their store last year, and I went to get a good deal on ammo. But the seminars were great too. Rob Downey, owner of Annamaet was a featured speaker. I asked him about high protein diets, and he told me that the prevailing opinion in veterinary science agrees with my vet. He also mentioned that the view that high protein causes kidney failure in dogs stems from one decades old study, which was an experiment on rats.

I worked in the Allegheny National Forest in the summer of 1988. I was a high school kid, and we were paid to improve trails, build fish habitat, blaze a new trail, girdle trees, and even fight a forest fire. Well, the fire was extinguished by the time we got there, but a ditch was being dug around the entire perimeter of the affected area. As soon as us high school kids showed up to dig the full time guys stopped digging, and we swung picks and shovels through roots and rocks to provide a buffer while the full time guys pointed at different things and walked around. It was a hot summer and I was packing frozen Gatorade in my lunch, which thawed by mid-morning and was warm by quitting time, but it worked well in that heat.

Gatorade works for people because we sweat and the beverage replaces electrolytes. Dogs don't sweat, and therefore do not need electrolytes, unless they are sick. Dogs lose electrolytes when they go to the bathroom—they do not use sweating as a means to cool down, and therefore they do not need electrolytes while working. Performance is better derived by understanding how a dog, which is basically a wolf in terms of genetics, functions. In fact, electrolytes can be harmful to a dog in sufficient doses.

Dog's burn glycogen that is stored in the muscles as a fuel when exercising strenuously. If you are training your beagles hard, they will deplete these stores of glycogen. I am not talking about a couple hours of chasing bunnies, but all day exercise; the kind of exertion a beagle might be doing in while campaigned in the field trial season or while being exercised heavily in the hunting season. If you can get that glycogen restored to your dog within two hours of exercise you will see improved energy the next day. I use *Glucocharge*, from *Annamaet*, and I buy it at Lion Country Supply. It gives you the dose for your dog, and it is a powder that can be dissolved in liquid at the time that you water your dogs at the end of a chase. I have used it this past hunting season when I was able to hunt for an entire week. I was more than surprised at the results. My beagles woke up every day ready to hunt.

Have a dog with bad breath? My old Rebel had a bad tooth removed, and it made his belches much less offensive. More importantly, his nose got better, or at least was as strong as it was when he was young. Taste and smell are closely related, which is why food doesn't have as much flavor when we have a stuffed nose. A rotten tooth will affect scent, especially in a dog, which has a sense of smell thousands of times stronger than ours.

"Do you brush your dogs' teeth?" my vet asked me after the tooth was extracted.

"Uh, well," I stammered, "am I supposed to? Is there something they can eat to fix the problem?"

It turns out there is, and while it is not supposed to be as good as brushing the teeth, I have decided that I will just go ahead and buy the teeth cleaning treats. Pedigree makes one called Dentastix, Milk Bone has a bone shaped product to clean teeth. AKC even sells a tooth cleaning snack. Some people feed bones to their dogs, but that results in diarrhea at my place—and my dogs are in the house. I use the Pedigree product, or sometimes those hard crusty pig ears. It keeps the sniffer strong as a dog ages.

Speaking of older dogs, Dasuquin is a joint supplement that I purchase from my veterinarian. It relieves arthritis in the old dogs and is basically Glucosamine Hydrochloride, Methylsulfonylmethane and chondroitin Sulfate. It really helps my older dogs move better, and Rob Downey, who led the nutritional seminar at Lion Country Supply, says that chondroitin can add two additional productive years to a working dog's career. That is a lot of rabbits!

Dog food, dental care, joint supplements, and sometimes glycogen are all part of my canine health care now. I realize that these things are a financial expense, but it is a priority for me. There are other places I could spend money. Eating a few more meals of rabbit at home and a few less meals in a restaurant goes a long way towards helping pay those dog bills. I also own less dogs than many beaglers, and I understand that this makes a difference in affordability. Maintenance is important. Now, if you will excuse me, I am going to change the oil in my wife's car. She said that the light came on in her car telling her to do so.

A Mile in My Shoes

There was a time when I would say dumb things to my wife, Renee, such as, "Aren't you ready yet?" or "If we left right now we would be late." The reason that these things should not be said is that generally we are going someplace that I would rather not go. Who cares if we are late? Sometimes I will even say things that intentionally delay the process of leaving the house, such as "Hey, you have a different red shirt that looks really nice. Do you still have it?"

Obviously she does still own the shirt, as well as every shirt she has purchased since she was a teenager. She then takes time (lots) to find every red shirt in her inventory and shows them to me. "Nah, now that I think of it maybe the shirt was more pink then red." There is then a frenzy to gather all the pink shirts, and I randomly pink one and say, "That's it!"

"Oh, well, I will have to pick different colored pair of slacks to go with this top," she will say while biting her bottom lip in concentration, "but I can do that!"

If we get to the event before it is over, we will certainly miss all of the time devoted to small talk and eating tiny sandwiches. We may miss substantially more of the function than that, as picking a pair of slacks is much more complicated than picking a shirt since it involves her contorting her body into various positions that allow her to see her own butt in a mirror.

Even if I do not interfere in the wardrobe selection process, my wife and I have totally different ideas about how to get ready for something. She will typically wash her hair, dry it, and then engage in a stylized ritual wherein she applies any number of moisturizers, scents, paint, and other cosmetics to her face. Bob Ross could paint an entire nature scene—complete with a sunset, mountains, autumnal trees, a river and waterfall, and maybe a cabin—

in a half an hour while using a paint brush of the same size that I would use to paint a barn. A half hour isn't enough time for my wife to get all of her tiny tools out of storage to begin. She owns a travel kit of cosmetics that may be too large to qualify as a carry-on bag at the airport.

In contrast, I generally require the amount of time necessary to run one of those sticky lint rollers over the clothes that I am wearing in order to remove the dog hair. This takes several minutes, unless I was napping with a beagle on my chest, and then I simply change clothes, as there is no way to correct a shirt that has been plastered in the white hair from a beagle belly. I choose the first shirt and the first pair of pants that I see.

Recently we encountered a new delay—dress shoes. "Nobody needs this many pairs of dress shoes," I said. "I own a black pair and a brown pair, and that covers everything." I resigned myself to the fact that she would need a lot of time to color coordinate her shoes with jewelry and clothing. I went downstairs and decided that I had time for a snack, as we would definitely miss those little sandwiches. Much to my surprise, I heard her walking around upstairs with a great deal of vigor. This is the sort of thing that must imply that she was trying all sorts of shoes and returning them to the closet before trying another pair. This was in contrast to the usual process of standing and staring at the shoes, and in theory waiting for said shoes to communicate with her or inspire a selection, much the way I might look at beagles in the morning and agonize over whether or not to take the young dogs for a chase or let the old timers have a chase. The loudest dogs persuade me.

I went to the kitchen, had a snack, and decided to have a short nap on the couch, when I heard her walking down the stairs. This would be the beginning of the process wherein she would interrogate me about the pair of shoes she was wearing. She would ask for my opinion.

I remember essay questions in high school English classes where the teacher might ask, "Which of Shakespeare's plays did you like best? Explain your answer." It was not enough to write "Macbeth." It was the explaining part that the teacher cared about the most, and your answer had to be more detailed than, "It had swords and a ghost."

Likewise, when asked a simple question such as, "Do you like these shoes?" a man should anticipate a follow up question that demands the rationale for liking or disliking any particular shoe. For the record, and answer of "I really don't care, just pick the pair that makes you happy" is woefully unsatisfactory. I was fully anticipating my shoe exam to be issued when I heard a noise that sounded like a drum roll. I sat upright on the couch and looked over to see that she had dumped all my hunting boots in a pile on the living room floor.

"No one who owns eight pairs of hunting boots should ever complain about how many pairs of shoes his wife owns." Renee stood barefoot (obviously she hadn't selected any shoes) with her arms crossed, waiting for my response.

"Well played, Mrs. Ford," I said. "Well played."

"Well," she sighed, "say something!"

"O.K.," I stalled to think of something to say. "How did you drop all those boots without hitting one of your feet?"

This was clearly not the response she was hoping for. I had considered explaining that eight pairs of boots is a very small number in comparison to her shoes, but then decided that such a reply would provide an opportunity to discuss the cost of my eight pairs of boots versus the price tag of her hoard of footwear. This was not a debate I wanted to enter, as I have some nice boots.

My favorite, for most of the year, is a leather lined pair of rubber boots. My feet get sweaty and itchy in many pairs of rubber boots. These ones have all the comfort of leather and the waterproof dependability of rubber. They are just perfect at the beagle club, as the bottom of the club property stays muddy and nasty all year long. These boots are also not subject to getting a hot foot, which is when you start the day on cool morning dew and before you know it the afternoon sun is beating down upon your rubber boots and your feet get so hot that you are looking for the closest mud puddle to cool them down!

Those boots aren't the best in cooler temperatures, and I also have a pull over boot that is rated to very low temps. I use them while deer hunting, especially if I am sitting still, but they are also nice for the January rabbit hunting season as well! Sometimes I may stand still in the snow while the hounds chase a rabbit for several circles before I manage to get a shot. Those warm boots sure are nice! I have another pair made by the same company that are rated for slightly warmer temperatures but are really nice for cold autumn mornings that may involve walking through water.

There are two pairs of leather boots that are nice in the afternoon while running after bunnies and trying to keep up with my beagles whenever we are finding pheasants or grouse. I have a beagle that will follow them, but he certainly won't point. In fact, he caught a perfectly healthy pheasant that was stocked by the game commission. The bird was semi-tame, and it wasn't smart enough to fly when Duke got close! Normally, however, Duke will flush them, and I can tell when he is chasing birds because he moves with all the vigor that he has when following a rabbit except for the fact that he is mute, or making muffled, high pitched barks on the bird scent. I have to stay close if I am going to get a shot, and those leather boots make it easier! Usually he doesn't go 40 yards before the bird is flushed, but if I am 40 yards away from a bird that moves even further, then my success rate is nil. One leather pair is a little warmer with some extra briar protection on the toe and heel, while the other is lighter and ideal for summer conditioning when I may run dogs in the evening and spend most of the time sprinting so as to keep myself between the dogs and any road that may pose a danger due to traffic.

There was a tall, zippered pair of bull hide boots that were snake proof. They are great for walking along small streams that have rocky banks with potential snake dens while catching native brook trout in the spring and are also my favorite boots for spring turkey season when the snakes are waking up for the summer. I also like them in the greenbrier, multi-floral rose, and other thorny places in the early rabbit season, since they have no laces to become untied in the brush, and unlike my other leather boots, these ones repel briars. I guess that would be expected if they have to protect a hunter from a timber rattler.

Another pair of boots that was on the floor is ideal for attaching to my snowshoes. The tread isn't the best for other things, but I sure do like the flexible support in my ankle when using snowshoes in brushy terrain. I could now understand what all that walking was that I heard upstairs—she was gathering all these boots from various closets and other storage spots.

"Well, say something!" she snapped me back to the moment as I was looking at the eighth pair of boots. I looked at that last pair and smiled. "What are you laughing at?" she grumped.

"I only have seven pairs of hunting boots. That other is a pair of hip boots for fishing," I said. I could tell you her response, but I try not to put much profanity in my column. I guess we all just have to walk a mile in each other's shoes.

Love Handles

My father had five kids to his first wife, and those kids were all adults by the time he was remarried to my mom. I never really saw much of those siblings, except for one brother (John) that worked in the same factory as Dad, and my sister Linda who did a lot of babysitting for my mom and dad when my father was constantly going to doctor visits for cancer. She also was the one who took me deer hunting when I was too young to legally hunt alone.

Dad was a deer hunter, for sure, but he would take all the work that he could get. If a guy wanted to be on vacation for deer season (someone always wants to be on vacation for deer season), then Dad would gladly wok a double shift every day that week for the overtime pay. A big deal is made about some people having to work holidays, but I think Dad worked all of them. We ate Thanksgiving whenever Dad got home from work. Or before he went to work. Or when he woke up after working all night. You see what I mean? Every holiday was like that.

So my sister Linda would often be the one to take me hunting. I remember one year shivering in the cold snow and bouncing a frozen stick off the ground in rapid succession like a drum roll trying to keep warm. This was in the days before goretex and thinsulate and all the great stuff, or at least before it was commonly available. In those years we wore the same clothes we always wore—but more of them. Long johns and sweat pants and blue jeans were combined to form a cotton wick that would draw all moisture directly to the back side. Eighteen shirts were worn for warmth, the top several layers belonging to my 6'2" father—but they fit perfectly on my 5'0" frame when stretched over all the tee shirts and plaid flannels and hooded sweat shirts.

"You know," Linda said, "a deer can probably hear that noise for miles." I stopped my drumming.

"S-S-S-S-sorry," I stuttered. The many layers of clothes had sponged the snow into my bones, and I was shivering.

"Let's go to the truck and get warm," Sis replied.

Linda's truck was really a candy store where everything was free. Snickers and Milky Way candy bars were in sacks in the back seat. Sandwiches and chips and hot cocoa were in abundance. The candy bars were always frozen. Sometimes you could set the candy bar on the defroster and try to thaw it, although there was a very narrow window between thawed and molten. In the spring, Linda also brought pounds of Easter candy to the house. She loved making the candy in various shapes—eggs, rabbits, baskets, ducks, and more. There was white chocolate, milk chocolate, chocolate with rice cereal inside, chocolate covered peanut butter and more.

My sister Linda had two daughters, Wendy and Fea, which is how her older brothers pronounced Fae. Her brothers are twins, Kim and Keith. They are six years older than me, which doesn't seem like much now, but back then it made them like older brothers, which is odd since they were my nephews. But my own older brothers were more like uncles—the ones you don't see very much. Wendy and Fea were closer to my age. I remember scraping together my Christmas tips from the paper route to buy a Remington pump .22 rifle. Dad was working overtime so Kim took me and signed the paperwork as my 13 year old hand put the wad of $5 dollar bills on the counter to get the gun. I still remember the shocked look from the clerk as the 19 year old Kim looked down at me and said, "That's a nice gun, Uncle Bobby." To avoid long explanations that are requisite in this circumstance we usually told people we were cousins.

Anyway, the twins were like big brothers. It is important to have big brothers so that you can learn how it feels to get teased, humiliated, pranked, and pummeled. Those things weren't very common. Mostly my nephews threw batting practice, took me fishing, and taught me about hunting. One or the other was always available. Oh, and Keith got a red and white beagle just a few years before I got my first beagle. We hunted rabbits all the time —or at least when they were home from college. The red and white beagle was cleverly named Red after mulling the possibilities over for a long time—maybe ten seconds. I shot my first hare in front of Red, before I got my own beagles. Red was a fixture in my hunting life, and after my dad and I got two beagles, we would often take Red and Duke together, as they were well matched in terms of their speed. My other dog, Princess, was much faster.

One day the unthinkable happened, and Red was run over by a milk truck. The driver kept on going and never stopped. The dog lived. In fact he had a lot of hunting seasons after that, but at the time his pelvis was smashed into 13 pieces, and the vet told my sister that the beagle was one of the best breeds for this accident, as their pelvis is somehow more able to heal from this sort of injury than a lot of other breeds. The milk company footed the bill, as I recall, as they were very saddened about the matter when Linda called them.

After a long stay in the veterinary hospital, Red went home and lived in the house, which was new for him. Linda babied Red, and under her care he became housebroken and whole. His biggest problem was going to the bathroom while he finished healing. He would hike a leg to pee and then he would fall over on the lawn as the leg muscles were still recovering. So, whenever Red would have to pee Linda would follow the dog into the yard.

As you know, a dog cannot simply pee. Sure, I know people that train their dogs to crap and squirt on command, but I have never found it particularly useful in a hunting dog. Most dogs need all the right surroundings before urinating. Women, I think, are like this too. When I got married, the bathroom was transformed into a room that looked like you might do anything there other than have a bowel movement. Fragrant containers of flower pedals and scented candles arrived. Previously, I had simply left the toilet paper sitting on the floor next to the commode. It was immediately elevated to the toilet paper-dowel-dookickey-dispenser thing. Oh, and it was a new brand of paper—much softer and thicker. My wife came with a stepson—a pre-fabricated family, and he would routinely clog the commode with this soft paper that seemed to expand like a sponge in the bowl.

The reserve roll of paper was not merely covered with the wrapper. When I was single, I bought the toilet paper one roll at a time. My wife purchases a massive container of paper that almost fills the shopping cart. These rolls (maybe 1,000,000 of them per package?) are not wrapped in paper, but all scrunched together in cellophane wrapping. There is always a full roll "on deck" which is to say the back of the toilet. It is covered in a cute little cover —I presume so that you are not looking at something as crude as toilet paper. But everyone knows what it is. Do they think that there is a pot of tea steeping under there?

Anyway, these are the things that are apparently necessary for my wife to pee. A dog needs to find the proper olfactory stimulation to relieve itself. The scent of another dog's pee is preferred. If such a thing is not available, the dog might wander aimlessly for minutes in the half-cocked position. This is where the dog keeps lifting a leg and then changes his mind and lowers it before ambling off on three legs whilst one hind leg is partially raised. Red had trouble with this maneuver, and Linda would follow him around the yard, walking alongside him while she bent at the waist so that when Red hiked a leg she could hold him up by letting Red lean against her hand instead of falling. She followed him around the yard hunched over like Groucho Marx—but lower—waiting for Red to pee.

A male dog is like a gunslinger in a cowboy movie—they never run out of ammo, never reload, and you wonder where they could possibly be getting all this urine as they wander around and scent mark every bush, tree, hydrant, pole, or yard ornament in the neighborhood. So Linda would make the rounds with Red as he reclaimed all of those items in his yard that had been claimed by other dogs that ambled through the lawn.

My nephew Kim is now retired from the Army and has a beagle named Riley. He moved back to his hometown, and Riley sees Linda often. Riley looks like a very fat Labrador retriever with a beagle head and feet. She is gigantic, even if she was in shape. Way taller than 15 inches tall at the shoulders, she was whelped in Colorado where the deep snows favor a longer legged hound. But she's overweight for sure. Kim and Keith must have the metabolism of hummingbirds to stay skinny through childhood. Riley moved into the house in her late middle age (canine years), and she never had a chance. She is content and very pleasant.

Last week I took Duke hunting with Riley. Not the same Duke I had as a kid, but a new one. He's young. But he is not my fastest hound, and I thought that would be better for Riley. Riley has a fantastic nose, but she was still not able to keep up with Duke. After the hunt we went to see Linda for supper and we ate well! Kim went out and brought Duke into the house from the truck before I drove home. Duke is not short—clearly a 15 inch-hound, but he is dwarfed by Riley. My sister's standard for how a beagle looks is Riley.

"He's so cute!" she cooed when Duke entered the house. "But the poor thing is emancipated! He needs food!"

"Do you mean emaciated?" I asked.

"Whatever, but he needs to eat!" And into the fridge she retrieved some roast beef that was just put in there after supper.

Duke enjoyed every morsel. It had been a lot of years since I ended a day of hunting at Linda's house. It was quite common when I was a kid. In the hectic days of modern life, we all have to step up and make sure that kids can get time in the woods. Probably very few of us were taken to the woods by an older sister. Fewer yet by nephews. I should have told Linda that I keep granola bars in the truck instead of candy bars. Damn things are still just as prone to freezing. I have to go run Duke. He seems to have put on a little weight. I think Sis calls them love handles. I know that love from Linda is part of why I am so active in the outdoors today. Thanks, Sis!

Vicarious

One of the perplexing realities about our sport is that we find people who take an odd sort of pride in being able to say that they owned a great dog. Often times they did not own the sire or the dam, and they were not the breeder of the great dog. We encounter this all the time at high school sporting events when a proud father stands up and says, "That is my son!" after a touchdown or goal. The exuberance is even more heightened if the father was not a talented athlete himself. It is clearly a case of nepotism, and the degree to which our society has encouraged this sort of behavior is astounding. I have witnessed unsportsmanlike conduct penalties at high school football games that were issued because of the poor behavior of the parents in the bleachers.

In the case of dogs, we are talking about the pride of owning a dog that is not our own progeny. The dog wins the prizes. Oh, the owner can do some things to help, but this mostly consists in getting the dog in shape—making the time required to give the beagle many hours of chasing rabbits. For the most part, however, the dog is the achiever. The owner merely paid for the pup.

This is perhaps not true when it comes to recognizing the breeder, who has decided what dam to mate with what sire. The breeder has a lot of responsibility in bettering the breed. Here again, however, we find that it is the pups that have to achieve. There is no shortage of great dogs that never passed their talent to the next generation with any consistency. There are fantastic beagles that are the perfect combination of recessive genes that all are evident and demonstrated in that hound, but those genes are not given to his or her offspring.

I am always impressed with guys that talk about hounds rather than people at trials. I find it to be a good trait in a person when he can recognize brilliance in a dog even if he does not like the owner or the breeder. It is the pettiness of competition that can sometimes make for field trials to be unpleasant. Someone ALWAYS spins the tires in anger when leaving a club after not making second series. I've seen fist fights narrowly avoided and heard of brawls that actually happened! I realize that a field trial is a competition, but it is the hounds that are competing, not us!

Actually, if the judges are any good, the dogs aren't really competing either except that they are all doing their best to move the rabbit. The pack is doing everything it can to chase the darn rabbit. The competition is amongst the owners and handlers of these hounds even though these people are actually spectators and not participants. The beagles are doing the hard work of running the bunny, and the judges are doing the unenviable task of evaluating the age old struggle of chaser and chased. It truly is a difficult job. It is hard to see the dogs in the brush. Your dog may do lots of wonderful thinks in the brush where the judges aren't sure if it is your hound or the other dog in the pack with a nearly identical voice. Oh, and my dog may make all of its mistakes when the judges can see it. Lastly, the judges have to explain themselves to all of the guys who do not win.

Of course, people are never happy with the explanation for why their hounds were picked up or did not advance to the next series. I've seen people furious about placing second! Hey, judges make mistakes—the good ones all admit that. Sure, it does happen that a dog should have placed better than it did on any given day, but it seems to me that the proper response is to disagree without an argument. The alternative is to be like those parents that earned unsportsmanlike penalties while they watched their kids play.

"It's because they never did anything in life!" a guy once told me about meaner spirited beaglers.

"What?" I replied.

"They never made the team as kids. They never graduated college. They never got a job that they liked. All they have is placing in field trials. There is nothing else for them," he laughed.

22

I thought about that. Could that possibly be true? I have never been a big fan of defining somebody on the basis of his job, but that is precisely what happens. People judge us based upon what we do for a living. My wife is constantly setting play dates for me. What I mean by that is she likes to go out to dinner with her friends, and they decide to make all their husbands go along too. The conversations all look the same.

"Hi, I'm Bob," and we shake hands.

"I'm Jim."

"Nice to meet you, Jim."

"You too. So, what do you do, Bob?"

Isn't that the natural progression of meeting strangers? We want to know what people do to pay the bills! I tell them I am a pastor and very often the conversation dies right there. Evidently that is a job that many people do not like. Or at least the husbands of my wife's friends. Hmmm, what kind of gals does my wife hang out with, anyway?

No, I like to think that we are people and not a resume. If I scan through my mental rolodex of friends (ah, that would be a mental cell phone list of contacts for you kids), I can see nothing in common amongst my friends in terms of vocation. Some work at a desk, and some work on a line. Some answer phones, and some drive ten hours per day. A few manage large sums of money, and some can't seem to pay the bills and keep the water turned on. They are all my friends because of who they are—not what they do for a living.

As a pastor I go to a lot of funerals, probably more than most people. The attendance at these things has very little to do with what the deceased did to pay the bills. You can have a great resume and still be a jerk. Friendships are rooted in something much more substantial than our jobs. Hey, I grew up in a town where everybody worked in the factory and almost no one liked their job! My dad worked 44 years in that factory and then died. Career was never a word I heard growing up. Work, yes. Job, certainly. Overtime—absolutely—my dad loved overtime more than I loved hunting! Not career though.

I was mulling over this notion that the meanest beaglers were the folks that accomplished the least in life. Could it be true? I caught myself at a trial last year trying to assess people on this guy's theory. It felt terrible to reduce someone to the things on their wall and shelves—certificates, diplomas, and trophies. How could I really know though? Sure, I know what a lot of the guys I see do for a living, but I have never been the best at figuring that out. I almost never ask a person where they work. If you are friends for any length of time, it will become obvious in conversation. I have many casual acquaintances for which I have no inkling as to their employment, especially beagle folks.

No, I don't know that I agree with the guy that thinks the meanest beaglers are somehow less accomplished people by worldly standards. But I do think that somehow these guys think that the dog is a reflection upon them. It is like they are living vicariously through the dog. I have friends that are devastated when their favorite sports team loses. They are living vicariously through those teams. Why are they so sad when the team loses? Why are they so emotional when they win? They are not employees of the franchise. And they aren't part owners of the team!

Maybe that is it. Maybe it is the ownership of the dog that makes folks so competitive with each other while the beagles are cooperating to chase the rabbit. I suppose football team owners look at Lombardi trophies as if they won them. I mean they did draft the players and sign their paychecks, but they never played in the games! When I talk to houndsmen that I appreciate I always find a different mindset in regards to owning a good hound—it is humbling and educational to own a good hound. It is a pleasure to watch a great beagle chase. A dog that won the genetic lottery is living in your kennel, and you feel lucky. Not full of pride—the dog is good—not you. But lucky to see such a fantastic "rabbit dawg" perform in the short time that they live.

BLINKS AND EYE ROLLS

I don't mean to brag, but I get called to the rescue by lots of people when they get their vehicles stuck in any number of settings. Plow into mud that is too deep? Are your tires off the road and on the ice? Manage to get your truck high centered, wherein its weight is resting on the differentials and the tires are dangling above deep ruts? Folks call me. Am I a master of off-road driving skill? Yes I am, but only if you define "master of off-road driving" as a person that has gotten themselves stuck too many times to count and managed to escape those situations with some damage to the vehicle through a process that could be labeled trial and error. Mostly error. I have required farm tractors to come get me on two separate occasions! I no longer have this difficulty, however, as I tend to be much more conservative in my driving and choose not to go places where I have doubts about my ability to return.

Not long ago, however, I managed to find myself stranded within an abandoned strip mine. Strip mines are some of the ugliest things you have ever seen from the air. Up close they are not exactly beautiful. There is no doubt that these mountain tops that have been excavated for the coal underneath will have great difficulty growing hardwoods again, if they ever grow trees. Often times, however, they will sustain scrubby brush, a variety of grasses, and some shallow rooted conifers. In other words, some pretty good rabbit habitat!

It is not uncommon for me to drive onto a hilltop mine that has been abandoned for a number of years, park the truck, stand beside the tailgate and think, "This looks like a beagle club where the membership doesn't do the best maintenance on their running grounds." In other words, these mines can be great cover. Last summer I trained my dogs in just such a place. The rabbits ran big circles with few tricks, and the music was beautiful. There were so many rabbits that I decided to hunt there a few times this season.

I may be the last outdoorsman who does not own an ATV. I am not sure about your hometown, but where I live it is not uncommon to see a $10,000 four wheeler in a driveway, parked right next to the $500 car that the guy uses on the highway. Most of my favorite rabbit hunting spots are full of four wheelers and the accompanying maze. By maze, I mean the multitude of four-wheeler trails that are created for the sole purpose of going around a mud puddle; the end result being that there are lots of detours that all return to the main road, and over the course of several rainstorms result in a single wide, muddy, rutty mess of a road.

I am told that the reason such mega-mud fields are made is because there are some casual ATV riders that do not want to get wet when they are out for a joy ride while wearing a pair of shorts. Over time it just makes a mess. Much of the time I curse these riders and the mess that is made—why can't we all just use the existing roads?

I had a successful hunt that ended as the snow began falling at an increased rate. I returned the way I arrived when I discovered that one of these mega-mud-traps that I just described was going to be a problem. It was at the bottom of a hill when I drove in, but it was now at the base of the same hill as I tried to go home. I put the truck in four-wheel-drive, my standard operating procedure being that when I need four-wheel-drive I go home. If two-wheel-drive got me here, than four-wheel-drive should get me out.

I was wrong. Luckily four-low was able to get me out of the mud, but only by retreating from the hill. I was going to have to find a new way out of this old coal mine. I turned around and entered the labyrinth of roads and four wheeler trails that looked like road-until they led into places that were too tight for a truck to follow. A large boulder had four different roads that branched out around it—two to each side. It was a good landmark, and I knew I could rely upon it to scientifically eliminate the roads that were dead ends or impassable.

The third time I passed the boulder, I decided to call home. "WHAT?" my wife answered. Caller I.D. can be a wonderful thing. She clearly knew it was me.

"I'm gonna be late for supper," I said.

"No kidding!" she rolled her eyes. I couldn't see her, but I am certain she rolled her eyes. Probably threw a hand in the air too.

"I can't get out of the woods."

"Stuck again?" She sounded like she was blinking now instead of rolling her eyes.

"Nah," I said. "Nothing that serious. I am just a little lost."

"Okay," she said. "What is a little lost?"

"I know what county I am in," I bit my lower lip as I looked out the windshield with the snow melting as it landed upon the glass, "and I know that I should be within 10 miles of a hardtop road."

"Are you going to be all right?"

"Oh, yeah," I said, "I still have a good half hour of daylight. I will call you if I get stuck." The good thing about being on top of a mountain is you have excellent cell phone reception. The next time that I called her, I was in a valley with one bar of reception and ended up texting her cell phone since I could get a text out much easier than a call. I told her I was doing fine. She texted back that she was getting ready for bed.

Finally, after passing that big boulder a couple more times, using the jack twice, and relying upon the fact that the rapidly cooling temperatures was making the ground frozen, and hence providing better traction, I managed to get out of the woods. I called home to give the good news. I drove a mere 7 miles to see a road sign that listed a highway I knew, and managed to pull into a gas station with at least 1/8 of a tank still in the truck.

I parked the truck at home an hour later as muck, mud, and snow dripped off the undercarriage. I brought the dogs into the house, and put the rabbits in the fridge to soak. My wife grabbed me and squeezed—no blinking, no eye rolling. "That must have been terrible," she said to me.

"Nah," I said as I patted her back. "Not once did I think I was so stuck that I needed a tractor to get me out. Besides, I think I found a couple good spots to hunt as long as the temperatures stay cold and the ground is hard." She stopped hugging me and started blinking.

Snow Shovels

My stepson sleeps till noon whenever they cancel school for snow. Lake Erie hasn't frozen as frequently as it once did, and it is not uncommon to get big accumulations of snow in March whenever the winds blow out of the northwest. When I was a kid, and there was even a rumor that school might get cancelled due to snow, I was awake before daylight shoveling our sidewalk and waiting for the snow to stop so I could go door to door soliciting the neighbors to hire my snow shoveling prowess. Five dollars was a typical pay from the houses that were big and had lots of sidewalks. Two or three dollars was more common from the smaller houses. I never set a price. I just said that they could pay me whatever they thought the job was worth. I once spent an hour on a sidewalk that only paid sixty cents. The sole resident was an elderly woman, who I think never married. She paid me in nickels, and no doubt remembered paying kids a few pennies during The Great Depression. I never went back there, but she would see me shoveling her neighbor's walk and come outside in her pajamas, "Yoo-hoo! Young man! You forgot me last time! Please shovel today!" So I would spend an hour digging out the narrow walks that crisscrossed her massive lawn, leading to sheds, a gazebo, a screen house, and a very fancy garden fountain. Oh well.

For reasons that I cannot explain, there are few kids doing such things today. As a result, I have to do much of the snow removal at my own house while our teenager sleeps the morning away. I have broken two shovels this year. I am still perplexed as to why they make the damn things out of plastic these days! They get brittle in cold air, and even though the really cold days produce a light, powdery snow, it is still easy to crack one. It wasn't too many decades ago that snow was shoveled with a coal shovel in these parts. If you can stab a shovel into rock

29

hard coal, you can move snow. These heavy implements doubled as ice choppers when a warm afternoon sun melted snow across the sidewalks before a cold north wind invaded overnight, covering the walkways and roads with a coating of ice. A coal shovel could smash the ice into jagged shards that could then be scooped out of the way. If you try to break ice with a modern shovel, you will fail. This is why I bought two shovels this year—and from trying to push too much snow.

Anyway, I love running rabbits in the snow and have always found that my best snow dogs will use their eyes as much as their noses—they look for rabbit tracks. I like to shovel the walk quickly and get out to the brush! I have a favorite hunting spot that is often frustrating. There is a large dirt pile that has been overgrown with burdock and grass. A lot of chases end there, as the mound is covered with groundhog holes. There might be a dozen holes there. I have put kids and old timers alike on that dirt mound since I know they will definitely get a shot at a rabbit. I will only shoot a rabbit there if the chase starts there, as I always let the bunnies circle at least once. More often than not, however, the rabbit is jumped somewhere nearby, and the chase will go for a half circle to that mound and end. Perhaps that is why there are always rabbits there, but some days the chases are very short and frustrating as a dog sticks his head in a hole and barks.

By February we had enough snow that I had to hunt that spot wearing snowshoes due to the drifting snow. Some days the beagle never fell through the crusty surface of the icy surface. One day I left the snowshoes in the truck, as the snow was so hard that I was barely making an imprint on the deep snow. The whole place looked like tundra, and the rabbits were running big! It was some of the best hound music of the season! Clumps of burdock, a stand of pines, and an area of thick saplings held most of the rabbits, and they provided fantastic hunts.

The snows continued. The local news makes a big fuss about an inch or two of snow. This wasn't always the case, and we just presumed that the moisture laden air that crossed Lake Erie would naturally fall in the form of a fresh powder at night as the temperatures cooled. Now it is trumpeted a big deal to get an inch of snow in order to make a news story. Some days this winter I could take care of the sidewalk between our house and the church parking lot with a broom—just push the light flakes to the parking lot like sawdust and leave it for the snowplow that would come eventually to scrape the lot. I did this chore quickly while my truck idled and defrosted the windshield, and then I would speed away to that wonderful hunting spot!

I broke the first shovel on a 31-degree day where the snowflakes looked like small snowballs and piled into a dense and heavy snow. The flimsy shovel was not made for the hectic pace I was using in order to rush off with the beagles. I finished the job with a garden shovel—not ideal. Within minutes of arriving at the dirt pile (snow pile at that point), I was no longer too dejected about the need to purchase a new shovel as the hounds roared into the pines on a fast chase. Besides, I could look for a good shovel. I stopped at the hardware store on the way home from that great hunt—the dogs waited in the truck, their noses sniffed and snorted through the ventilation holes in the dog box to get the scent of that day's bunny harvest that was in the bed of the truck.

Cheap plastic or cheap lightweight aluminum were the two choices in shovels. Cheap is a reference to the quality, not the cost. I opted for cheap aluminum at an outrageous price. The fantastic hunts just kept coming as I would do the morning shovel and then shuffle of to that wonderful hunting spot. The dogs were really finding their stride when I mangled the second shovel. Some ice had formed overnight and the process of trying to break and/or lift the ice had bent the shovel in any number of directions. At one point the capacity of the shovel was halved because I managed to bend a big convex bubble into the middle of the shovel. The garden shovel made a return and I was in such a hurry that I threw the thing into the bed of the idling truck as I went to the woods.

Coyote tracks were all over my hot spot. And so were some cat tracks—the housecats that go wild. I found quite a bit of rabbit fur and blood. I had more great chases, and I suddenly noticed that all of them ran in the vicinity of the dirt pile. They wanted to get underground but couldn't due to the hard snow. I drew a bead on an easy rabbit that was quartering away from me from left to right. It bounded towards the dirt pile and then out of sight for a romp into the pines. I just couldn't shoot it. I unloaded the gun and took it to the truck. I grabbed the garden shovel and found five groundhog holes that I have routinely seen the dogs shove their heads into while hunting that spot. I couldn't find any other holes, but I know they are there. It took over an hour to find them, but it felt good.

I have been back to that spot, and the rabbits are going underground pretty quickly, now that they can. Sure, I can guarantee you that I will go back there next year and shoot rabbits. I may even shoot a few more this year before the season closes. I know that when the snow recedes I will locate some more of those holes in order to mentally map them so as to be able to shovel them out next winter. I can't put an exact price on what that hunting spot means to me. It is close to home, far from paved roads, and full of bunnies. How do I put a dollar value on that? If I could shovel for sixty cents an hour as a kid, then shoveling for these rabbits that provide so much to my beagles and me was a very lucrative job indeed.

TALK SHOWS AND THE INTERNET

Years from now, when the historians decide to document the decline of western culture, I am certain that it will begin with Phil Donahue. He, as I can remember, was the first sappy talk show that talked about people's problems in a way that was more entertainment than help. It then progressed to Oprah, Jerry Springer, and Dr. Phil. No doubt there are others. I have memories of being subjected to Donahue when I was a little kid and home from school sick. I would be lying if I said that my mom watched television. What would be more accurate is to say that she would listen to certain shows while she darted about the house cleaning, cooking, and being the chief financial officer. She wrote the checks to pay the bills and keep things running. If my father would have walked into the bank to cash his paycheck, they would not have known who he was. He brought the check home, signed it, and mom took it to the bank and deposited the money into the savings account.

Anyway, in addition to a soap opera, mom also listened to this Donahue guy. Those were the two shows she listened to as if they were a radio program. I had pneumonia as a baby and was subject to repeated bouts of bronchitis as a kid. When I was home from school due to illness, I hung over the edge of the couch and inhaled misty fog from a vaporizer that would loosen the mucus in my lungs and allow me to have "productive coughing," which is code for viscous phlegm, or what we kids called a "hocker." My apologies if you are eating supper. Vaporizers no longer seem to exist, and sick children are now taken to the emergency room every day until they are better. This is because moms and dads both have to work (whether they want to or not) and parents worry about kids that they do not see during the day. Also, doctors like to ensure a steady flow of cash. This was the old days, and I can recall that mustard plasters were put on my chest, and a substance called "black salve" applied to wounds.

I once was coughing and gagging and out of breath during an episode of Donahue and crawled to my shoes and coat, which I put on over with my pajamas. The pajamas had stains made by flat ginger ale. Mom thought flat ginger ale was good for a cold, and it was often given as a chaser for the nasty tasting medicine that was given by the tablespoon at certain intervals. "What are you doing?" Mom yelled at me as I zipped my coat.

"I'm feeling better." I hacked, "I think I can make the last bit of school." Donahue had healed me.

"No," she shook her head, "you will miss at least another day. Probably two."

That show just grated my nerves. It was a rejoicing in sorrow. It fed upon the worst tendencies in people. I knew that, even then. I think the same is true about internet beagling. Here me out! Discussion forums, social media, and an abundance of websites have allowed the beagling community to come together in remarkable ways. The internet allows us to communicate with people that have the same passions that we do about the merry beagle, and I have met great friends through those venues. It is, however, a place that tends to cater to the meaner side of our personalities. Some poor sap has a great day in the field and his pack of dogs is running well—so he whips out a cell phone and films some of the chase. He goes home and perhaps no one there cares about his great day. Not everyone has a wife that enjoys talking about hounds as much as my Renee.

"Honey, the dogs looked awesome this morning!"
"Great."
"The pup looks fantastic and is learning fast!"
"Wonderful."
"Would you like to go with me Saturday morning and watch some good hound work?"
"You don't say."
"I did say. Are you listening to me?"
"That's good to hear."

Most beaglers are not as fortunate as me and do not have a spouse that talks with them about beagles, and therefore they post the video online and caption it with a happy sentence such as "They ran great today!" Then the comments upon the video flood cyberspace. They start with things like "Terrible" or "Why do you own those dogs?" Next come statements upon the camera skills. "Can't see much but they look slow" and "Why are you filming dogs that are useless?" At this point the comments cease to be kind, and head towards darker thoughts that question the guy's manhood, intelligence, sexual orientation, and paternity. The internet can be a crude place.

No doubt many judges have wanted to say critical things about a dog when the owner, obviously upset, asks why the dog did not even place in the trial, let alone win as it deserved. The judge may want to say that the dog was not very good, but at this point the answer is something like, "Your dog didn't do anything wrong; it just didn't have enough score" or, "That dog just ran too much rabbit." Perhaps it is the personal contact that makes folks empathetic to the owner's feelings. Or the maniacal look that some fellows get when their dog doesn't win—they get less angry if you insult their kids' intelligence or question their wife's fidelity. The guy complains to other competitors that competed that day, and no one disagrees with him or brandishes a mean comment. "Better luck next time" and "I hear what you are saying" fill the air.

Does the computer make people meaner than they are? Maybe it just allows people to be more honest behind a screen name. I myself have maligned the traditional brace style of beagle on the internet by pointing out that they are too slow to circle a rabbit before the scent gets too cold to trail, but I also point out that this is what those guys desire in a dog. I try to make it a philosophical disagreement on rulebook interpretation, but I am sure slip in the occasional zinger.

Sometime ago I was informed that a gal I grew up with was going to be on Dr. Phil. I was told the day, time, and channel to find the program that featured her problems. As a pastor I have changed the channel in countless hospital waiting rooms when shows like Dr. Phil or Jerry Springer are being televised. No one needs to be subjected to a woman storming off a stage as she learns that the genetic test done on the umpteenth man from her past proves that he is also not the father of her baby. These shows seem mean spirited and petty. I look for *Sesame Street* or something like that.

I happened to be in front of a TV and saw the gal that I have not seen in 25 years right there in front of Dr. Phil. Who would want their problems hung out for the world to see? Are these guests paid to be there? The host made comments intended to insult the people on the stage while garnishing laughs from the studio audience. It was misery as entertainment. I turned off the boob tube and walked away long before the show was over.

When it comes to our traditions as owners of hunting beagles, I am very pleased with the fact that we have gundog federations, bloodlines, and clubs. The Triple Challenge at the historic National Beagle Club in Aldie, Virginia ties us to something bigger than ourselves. International field champions show our commitment to competition and bettering the breed. Even so, we are a small community. There are fewer hunters every year. Clubs struggle to survive. Gasoline prices make field trials cost prohibitive. We ought to encourage one another. We live in a country with suburban sensibilities that values neither hunting nor hunting dogs in many sectors. Let's work together to make sure our sport has a long future.

Further Conspiracies Involving the Easter Bunny

My ongoing battle with the Easter Bunny continues. Many years ago I wrote a piece that is probably best classified as an expose. I had discovered that the Easter Bunny was secretly conspiring with the American Dental Association to encourage cavities in kids and thus produce revenue for the dentists. It garnered no national attention, and the story was not even considered for the Pulitzer Prize or any journalistic awards. Indeed, one of my readers accused me of making the entire story up out of thin air, saying that the Easter Bunny is "not real" and that I had a tendency to exaggerate, use hyperbole, and tell lies. I found those comments hurtful, especially since I try to support my wife in all of her endeavors and she could at least do the same regarding my work.

Anyway, the Easter Bunny is intent on the doom of our dogs. He had once communicated with me via email that he intended to poison all beagles in retaliation for the hours of chasing that rabbits receive daily from hunting beagles. The poison he planned on using was chocolate. If you are anything like me, you may be shocked to learn that chocolate is indeed poisonous to dogs. I had a dog eat a whole bag of Halloween chocolate that was meant to be given to the costumed kiddos, and all it did was give the beast better smelling burps. Incidentally, I am currently working on a separate investigative piece that shows two things: (1) The Easter Bunny is also in collusion with companies that make Halloween costumes in an attempt to proliferate more chocolate caches being found in people's homes in order to endanger beagles and (2) The Easter

Bunny has also formed an alliance with Cupid. Both Cupid and the Easter Bunny, of course, are symbols of fertility, but the Easter Bunny made a bargain wherein women will accept chocolates as a gift from their valentines instead of the more expensive jewelry. Naturally, this arrangement works to the Easter Bunny's advantage by increasing the potentiality of beagles being exposed to chocolate. I have to thank my wife for this insight, which she discovered on the internet and then told me. She knows that I am aware of the Easter Bunny's hatred for beagles, and I now buy her expensive jewelry instead of chocolate! That'll show him and the winged baby that I am serious about this matter. Who is the fool now?

Chocolate really is poison to dogs, but the more common milk chocolate is not as potent as the dark chocolate or baker's chocolate. My veterinarian prescribes a simple fix for any occasion where a dog might ingest chocolate—give the dog a turkey-baster of hydrogen peroxide every few minutes until the mutt vomits the contents of its stomach—including the candy wrapper, or more likely the wrappers. This is best performed in a cage-match setting that would make for profit-making pay per view television wherein the dog cannot escape and vomit where you can not verify the results. A bathtub with a sliding door that prevents the dog from vacating the area works best. Also, dog vomit tends to attract other dogs. You want to isolate the guilty dog in the bathroom. Closing the toilet lid and removing the 432 items that your wife has precariously balanced on the shower/tub shelves is also highly recommended. For a 20 pound beagle you will need two adults, minimum, to control the dog and force the hydrogen peroxide into the stomach of your pooch. You would think that a dog that relishes the occasional snack of decaying carcass or rabbit turds would gladly drink some hydrogen peroxide, but they do not. You will need assistance. My wife helps me. Once you are assured that the medical emergency has passed, you can simply take off your clothes and shower away the dog slobber, chocolate, hydrogen peroxide, and hair. The dog hair isn't nearly as distressing as the sight of your own, as it was ripped from the scalp in the melee. As a veteran of such wars, I recommend that you apply a little hydrogen peroxide to the scratches on your arm as a disinfectant before you shower. Dog nails scratch deep. My wife's nails dig even deeper as she grabs my arm to keep from being thrown to the ground as a bloated beagle ricochets off my chest and into her side. Also, you may think you have seen some fairly enthusiastic vomiting gyrations from a dog. No doubt you have. As a way of providing a cautionary warning, however, I would tell you that no words I know (or anyone else) can adequately prepare you for the spectacle of a beagle with a belly full of hydrogen peroxide. The sounds alone are staggering, let alone the end results. It is quite shocking how powerful a beagle can be. Maybe it is the sugar rush from the candy.

Over the years, I have tried many times to stop this dreaded event. We told my stepson to keep the chocolate in his room. He did, storing it on the floor, with the bedroom door open. We insisted that the chocolate be kept in the kitchen cupboard so it could be monitored. The same chair the child used to reach the candy was utilized by the dogs with equal dexterity, perhaps even more. The child is a teenager now, so we are hoping that the problem has passed.

So, as I was saying, the Easter Bunny has decided to escalate the war. He now claims that his goal is to entice my dogs to run towards hazards—the road. The blasted bunny knows that I have always avoided training dogs or hunting near roads. He has encouraged his lagomorph brethren to propagate in great numbers during the spring and to entice our hounds to follow them through the yards. Perhaps, like myself, you have also ran over your fence in bare feet on a cold soggy lawn to catch your dogs as they have escaped under the yard's fence in order to chase after the rabbits that have turned your neighborhood into a bunny brothel.

I've had some fantastically crazy foot pursuits in the spring. The old timers swear that the doe rabbits emit less scent when they are pregnant or nursing. I can believe that —but the buck rabbits are just as enticing as they can be. Boy, do they travel long distances when breeding season arrives too. Sometimes you see them on the road, life ended to soon by a Buick as their passions burned hot. Nothing is more startling than letting your dogs out into the fenced yard for the last bathroom break of the night (we call that last call around my house) and hearing a sight chase erupt immediately that is only briefly interrupted by the sound of rattling chain link as the pack squishes under the fence where the retreating frost heaved the fence when it vacated the ground. The soft glow of neighboring houses and distant lights reveals a bouncing puff of white as the rabbit's tail heads for cover. For the record, I can still hoist myself over a 5 foot high chain link fence with ease, though my landings are a little rough these days. Especially in my moccasin slippers.

Given the far reaching effects into society that the Easter Bunny has influenced—Halloween, Valentine's Day, collaboration in making cavities—I am surprised that he has any respectability left. Perhaps his greatest crime of all is detracting our attention from the true meaning of Easter and focusing it upon candy and baskets. Oh, I am not a complete party pooper—I like fun times too. Peanut butter filled chocolate eggs are one of my favorite seasonal treats. I just hope that we can all take time to be thankful for the return of spring (we had an old fashioned winter here in Pennsylvania) and see the great joy of Christ and all that his resurrection brings to us. As the forests and fields regain their greenery, it is a foretaste of the eternity we are promised. Happy Easter. I have to go inspect my fence.

INFIDELITY

Infidelity is not a subject to be taken lightly. Who can say what causes such lapses in the judgment of men? It must be passion, burning deep within the soul that propels us to make decisions that ultimately result in conflict, commotion, and catastrophe. Worse yet, some men are repeat offenders, never learning their lesson and falling from grace on repeated circumstances. I find myself in the grips of such indiscretion at this time every year. I am talking about trout season, of course. What were you dirty-minded beaglers thinking?

I consider myself a houndsman, which is to say that beagles are my primary outdoor passion. I hunt most days of the hunting season for at least a couple hours, condition dogs all year, and when I travel out of state for a hunting trip it is always for rabbits or hare. Fido is a generic name for a dog, and its origins go to the root of the word, *fides* or faith. Our dogs are faithful! Well, I have made the argument that beagle loyalty could be purchased with the smallest morsel of food. I could use a small treat and your beagle could become mine, and you could do the same with my beagles. Sure there are a few beagles that are the exceptions that prove the rule, but there never seems to be any trouble getting a hound to perform for another handler at a trial—as long as they have rabbits (the only thing that overrides the desire for snacks) they are happy.

Anyway, I am unfaithful to my dogs in deer season and trout season. Those are the times of year when I leave the house with no hound and no briar pants. I still leave before dawn, and those mutts are accustomed to going with me at that time to drive to a hunting spot or a beagle club. I am not convinced that they even know that I own the truck. It could be that they view it as their magic box wherein they jump inside, and when they jump from the dog box they are surrounded by an abundance of briars and bunnies. I can tell you that they can hear my truck from a ½ mile away. When I return from work, they begin acting crazy a few minutes before I return. I never come home at the same time, so it can't be a matter of conditioning, as it is with dog food—always dispensed at sundown. My wife began calling me whenever they started acting crazy on my commutes home.

"Hello?" I answered.

"Where are you?"

"Almost home," I replied.

"I thought so!"

That above conversation happened a few times, and we discerned that ½ mile away was about the outer range of their ability to hear my truck. Interestingly they do not do the same with my wife's car—not even when I drive it. According to my research staff (a friend with the internet), a dog can discern one vehicle and detect particular sounds that are specific to that vehicle, and pick the tell-tale sounds out of the hundreds of cars that are passing the home. If my truck has a squeaky belt, the dogs can distinguish it from other squeaky belts. In other words, my dogs associate the sound of my truck with chasing rabbits. This is problematic when I leave the house in pursuit of trout at five o'clock in the morning. My wife is not what you would call a morning person.

There was a time when I would keep my fishing gear in the truck for the entire season and then scatter a few hands-full of dog food on the kitchen floor in the pre-dawn hour in order to distract the dogs while I sprinted to my vehicle, as if it were a Le Mans start in an auto race, so I could drive out of hearing. As long as they were eating, they could ignore the sound of my truck leaving the house without them. I presume that they then scoured the house for more kibbles and went back to sleep.

The problem was that the dogs began to gain weight—it takes a lot of food to occupy their attention till I can escape the ½ mile radius. Additionally, there are evenings in trout season when I may take the beasts to the beagle club to chase while I do paperwork and compose my weekly sermon. Most of my colleagues in ministry do paperwork and homily crafting in an office where there are desks, computers, and restrooms. I do have a similar office at the church, but it comes equipped with a telephone, wildly variable temperatures based upon the whims of a thermostat that I haven't located in 13 years of serving the parish, and two windows that make me wish I was outside. I much prefer to do such sedentary tasks on a beagle club porch while the pack sings. As a firm believer in not running dogs on a full stomach, I would rather not give them such a large amount of kibbles in the morning if they are going to chase that night.

So, last trout season, I bought one of those plastic, hollow, balls that are designed for holding dog treats. The outer surface of the ball has a few holes in it, and those holes, barely larger than the treats that you stuff through them, allow the tasty snacks to re-emerge when your beloved pet carefully manipulates the ball so that the snack can align itself in the proper direction and thus permit the crunchy reward to fall to the floor as a reward. Actually, I bought two of these things—to occupy the attention of the whole pack. They were only used once.

I placed the snack spheres on the ground and began my sprint, truck key in hand, fishing hat on my head. As I have said in my signed deposition to the marital court (my wife is both prosecuting attorney and judge), I can't be sure I heard any crashing sound as I closed the exterior house door behind me. I did hear a lot of barking, and this may have drowned out the sound of the lamp smashing on the floor. I also do not dispute the fact that my wife did call my cell phone, but it was on the vibrate setting, and I was listening to the radio. As also evidenced in the deposition, I did see the 34 missed calls that my cell phone registered while I was fishing—but only after I emerged, with great success I might add, from the trout stream I was visiting that particular morning. I had left the phone in the cup holder of my vehicle so that I could multitask while fishing—there is a great deal of "thinking time" while fishing, and this is one of the great joys of the sport. What an excellent aide in writing a message for the congregation. I did, however, see the missed calls when I grabbed the phone to take a picture of my catch in order to text it to a friend of mine who thinks I am a lousy fisherman.

I think my wife was exaggerating when just the other day, she said, "It sounded like wolves, felt like an earthquake, and still haunts my dreams to this day."

"Didn't they exercise their minds getting the treats out of the ball?" I asked. "I think the advertising said that. It said 'hours of fun,' or something like that."

"You ever see those cute cat videos on the internet?" she interrogated.

"No."

"Well this was the opposite. They moved the furniture! They shoved those balls through the entire house and were running very fast, but they couldn't corner at those speeds on the hardwood floors, so they would skid on their sides whenever the balls rolled away from them. That made them bark even louder until they came to a stop and started running at the balls again."

"Sounds like quite a scene," I said.

"It woke me!!" she yelled.

"Yeah, that must have been pretty loud," I said. My wife can sleep through alarm clocks.

"It woke Wes!" she said in a voice that might be used to announce some fact or statistic that is beyond comprehension. Wes, my stepson, is a teenager and at the peak of his sleeping abilities. There are very few things that can make him wake up. I once needed him to get out of bed to help me take a dog box out of my truck. I lied and told him that some pretty girl was at the door wanting to talk to him. He hasn't fallen for that trick again.

"One dog had a ball pinned against a corner in the living room so it couldn't roll away and kept bashing it off the wall to make treats fall out. Another dog stood close by to try and eat them before the basher could scarf them up."

"Nice!" I exuded. "You needed to film that. All the dog experts say the beagle is not intelligent. That is the documented proof we needed."

The reason we were discussing that event recently was because trout season is about to descend upon us again, and I need a new technique. One that lets her sleep while I fish. I suggested the only logical solution—we switch vehicles for trout season. The dogs don't associate her 4 cylinder sport utility vehicle with chasing rabbits. I can put

all my fishing gear and boots in the spacious back seat. It
really is a perfect plan. The judge of marital court
dismissed it.

Late for Supper

I have to confess that I have been in a little hot water with my wife, Renee. She and I are both employed, and we both have meetings on some evenings. For some reason, she seems to know the days and times of all my meetings and I, apparently, do not know any of her similarly scheduled functions. "I have them programmed into your calendar!" she yelled at me.

"Clearly not," I paged through my calendar.

"No," she rolled her eyes, "I did not say that they were written down on paper. They are programmed. Click on the calendar app on your phone."

"I don't know how to use that," I declared simply. She maintained eye contact with me (okay, it was a glare), and she grabbed a red ink pen with which she wrote the times of all her meetings into my calendar, which was impressive considering the fact that she never stopped staring at me.

At issue here is the fact that I have been running dogs over the supper hour. My stepson, a teenager, goes to an extracurricular activity after school every day. So there is no family supper—the school district has encroached upon every day of the week and every possible time. There are kids in the church where I pastor that routinely are driven several hours on Sunday to play soccer, bypassing plenty of other schools that also have soccer teams. They can't stop in those closer towns because those youngsters are also travelling two hours to a game. So I was sitting at home and eating sandwiches alone at 5 p.m. while my wife was waiting to get the kid at the school at 6 p.m. before getting takeout for her and the kid, as I would then leave for my 7 p.m. meeting as they were returning. There had to be something better, right?

So, I would run dogs, skipping supper, walking around the club property, listening to hound music, and conditioning the beagles. On the nights when I had meetings I would need to take precautions to keep my clothes clean. When I catch my dogs while they are running a hot line, I tend to resemble a trout that has just been thrown on a grassy bank, if the trout also had wildly flailing arms and legs. You can't walk into a church meeting with your clothes plastered in mud and grass stains. Similarly, you can't change clothes in the club parking lot either—that is when someone would show up to run dogs. So, I wore brush chaps over my dress pants, a long coat to cover my shirt, and placed a pair of shoes to exchange for my boots in the truck. Perfect.

Here is where the problem arose. On nights when I had no meetings I just went to the club in my standard bibs and let the dogs roll until well after dark, and I did this on nights when my wife was home. I did not know she was home because this was before she "programmed" my paper calendar, and she just presumed I knew the schedule written on my phone. All of this prompted a session of marital court. Marital court, by the way, is when Renee serves as both judge and prosecuting attorney, and I have no representation. Basically I am there to receive punishment, and my side of the story may (but probably not) present mitigating circumstances that could potentially reduce my sentence. At one time, I tried to base my defense in things like facts. I would have, in this instance, given dates and times of nights when no one came home for supper except me, presented evidence verifying that I ate leftovers while the judge and the kid ate in a restaurant because he didn't want to eat what we were having, and cited situations where school activities ended but were immediately followed by extended social interactions with peers (requiring a ride somewhere). I was married a long time before I determined that facts were irrelevant in marital court. Verdicts, in fact, are dispensed purely on the basis of emotion.

I discovered this by accident during case number 1124 when I was found guilty of letting dogs in the backseat of her car with no dog crate. In the cross examination, it came out that I was merely saving money (my truck is a gasoline hog) in order to buy her a birthday present. Granted, there was no acquittal, but the punishment was relatively minor. I decided to try the same thing with the whole criminal case that involved missing supper to chase rabbits.

"I got tired of eating alone, and I thought maybe with your busy schedule we would eat a late supper together when I got home. It's lonesome eating alone," I pouted and hung my head. It worked—a full pardon. In fact, she now is willing to bring supper and the kid to the beagle club so that we can eat it together while the dogs are circling rabbits. A picnic of sorts!

In my childhood things were different. My mom did not have a job. My dad was old fashioned and did not think moms should have jobs. Before you label him a sexist pig, you should also realize that he felt it was fine for a mom to have a career. The distinction, of course, was that jobs were places you went to make money while being miserable. My father worked for such a place. He worked there 46 years and died, before he ever received a pension. Once, a piece of machinery exploded and covered him with second and third degree burns. He got burned because the factory had opened the panels of the machinery, exposing the inner wiring that was behind them. This was done to try to cool them down, as they would overheat and shutdown. Opening the panels to expose the wires was what passed as maintenance in the factory. The factory never even paid for the clothes that had to be cut off his body, apologized, or said a word. Well, he was spoken to privately and told that if he complained or sued he would be out of a job and so would all of his relatives that worked there. Months later, after the wounds healed, he went back to work. That's a job.

Careers are places you go to do work that you enjoy. Such work might even provide fulfillment, a sense of accomplishment, and self worth. My mom did not have a career or a job. Instead, she worked all day, for no money, taking care of her family and home. She ran errands, did the shopping, and handled the finances. I do not remember seeing my father go to the bank once. He gave Mom his paycheck and kept a few dollars for gasoline and other things. This was back when a few dollars could fuel an 8-cylinder truck all week! This was in the old days when housewives were fairly common place, when one job could pay the bills for a family. My mother cooked supper every night, and no one was permitted to miss it, eat in front of the television, or read a book during the meal. The book rule was instituted for me, and she called the librarian so that she could give me additional warnings and threaten to examine any book I borrowed for food stains. The librarian wagged a finger at me while looking at me over her glasses, rather than through them. No one would have guessed that the day would eventually come when book stores would serve you full meals and hot beverages to consume whilst you read stuff you were never going to buy.

Beagling took place before or after meals. We would eat supper before I leashed the hounds to walk to a nearby running ground near a stream. Oftentimes my father and I would drive to the nearby beagle club and enjoy an evening of hound song. Mom never much cared to go to the woods with dogs, other than in blackberry season. That is when she would go to the beagle club with us in order to fill a bucket. The running grounds were full of berries, and she would give me and the pooches a ride when they were ripe. Dad changed shifts at the factory, and he worked some evenings.

Trips to the veterinarian were also something that fell under my mother's jurisdiction. Anything from annual check-ups, vaccinations, porcupine encounters, and one case of parvovirus were all handled by her. She made flour gravy in the winter and added lots of hot water to go with it in order to make sure that the dogs got enough fluids in the winter. She poured it over the dry dog food, forcing them to drink it in order to finish their food—but they loved every drop! I changed the water in the kennels before school, after school, and at feeding time, but the water would often freeze anyway.

She was the enforcer, making sure that I cleaned the kennels and tended the dogs as I said I would do when I begged to get them. She would also cover for me if I had some other task. Once, when I was in ninth grade, my dad had a lot of overtime. Father's ears perked up when he heard the word "overtime." The factory where he had his job had a simple plan whenever someone went on their vacation—somebody had to work extra. Dad volunteered for the extra. There were many weeks when he worked 16-hour days. He took every advantage of these opportunities as the additional hours paid a higher wage.

"I thought your job was no fun?" I asked.

"It isn't," he replied.

"So why do you go there for 16 hours of misery?"

"Rainy days. You need a little something for rainy days."

There was one November when dad worked three continuous weeks of overtime—right in the middle of rabbit season! There was no hunting to be done, as I was not yet 16, the age when the Game Commission deemed you safe enough to hunt alone. I had relatives that would often take me, but they often had to work on Saturdays too. They did not have a career; they had jobs. Jobs do not care about your schedule. In order to stay compliant with the law, my mom took me afield so that I was not hunting alone. To be fair, she sat in the car and waited for me to get finished, but she was there, though not within the legal proximity that the law required.

Mom also made sure that I did not get too excited about the woods and rivers. If my grades slipped, even a little bit, I was forbidden to hunt, fish, or even take dogs to chase rabbits. She insisted that I make every effort to not have a life typified by 16-hour work days. When Dad died, she had to go to work. I was in college, and she sold Princess, our best dog, for a tidy sum of money. The dog was in Dad's name. She did not sell Duke, which was in my name. Duke was old and died when I was a senior at college. I heard that the guy who bought Princess accidentally killed her by dropping something on her back while working in the yard. For a long time, I was upset at Mom about this. I understand now, however. The rainy day fund from the overtime ran out. It rained a lot after Dad died. Her job paid minimum wage.

I work as a pastor now—a career (a calling, in fact). I love what I do, and people share the difficult circumstances of their lives with me on a daily basis. My mom has since passed away, and there isn't a day that goes by when I am not thankful for all that she did—helping me to enjoy hounds, making sure I went to college, and ensuring that I could enjoy even my toughest days at work. In the end these beagles that we enjoy so much are not a substitution for our families. But if you can get your family to eat a picnic with you in the woods while the hounds are singing, go for it! I have to work on my pouting and sad look. I may still be late for supper once in a while.

In or Out

"Make up your mind! In or out!" my mom yelled at me one day when I was 6 or 7 years old. Okay, she yelled it many days. I was never good at staying indoors. When the skies would open and the rain would pour, I would go out on the porch and look to see if it was going to end soon. Then I would walk back in the house and lament the fact that it had not let up. So, I would walk out onto the back porch hoping to get a better view of the sky so that I could try and determine how long I would be confined to the house. This was before the Weather Channel existed. This was before you had unlimited access to meteorological radar maps on a computer. This was when computers were the size of a wealthy man's living room! The result of my pacing between the porches was a steady "THWAP!" from the screen door. Oh, and a certain amount of houseflies would get into the house as well.

My dad worked in a loud factory and couldn't really hear the screen door slapping shut. Dad couldn't hear a lot of things, actually. He always kept a fly swatter nearby and could knock one out of the air. "Where are all these darn flies coming from?" he yelled, though he may have felt he was whispering.

"From your son opening the doors every five seconds!" Mom answered.

"What are you talking about?" Dad yelled. He was trying to yell, so it was a bellow. "The sun ain't even shining! It is pouring out there! How could the sun bring bugs in the house anyway?"

My parents then engaged in a conversation that made no sense, mostly because Dad couldn't hear and Mom had no patience for his hearing loss.

"Why can't I go outside if I wear a raincoat and boots?" I asked.

"Fine," Mom said, Dad shot a double—knocking two flies out of the air with one sway. "Get out! Don't come back in!"

Ever heard someone described as not being smart enough to come in out of the rain? I caused that proverb to come into existence. I often hear the debate about beagles. Inside the house or outside?

As a pastor, I never know when the bishop might tell me to move to some other parish. I have been in the same spot for thirteen years, but I know that I am not in control of my residence. So, I decided to make hunting house beagles, as I was not willing to build an expensive kennel when I will have to move someday. There are pros and cons to this lifestyle. I will start with the cons.

Have you ever seen a couple, expecting their first child, make their home safe for youngsters? They put plastic plugs in the electrical outlets. They put child locks on the cabinets and refrigerator. They try to make the furniture be arranged so that their progeny cannot climb everything under the sun! New parents panic every time the toddler slips or skins a knee, running to scoop Junior into their arms and rock away the tears. The second kid is not so pampered. "Get up!" they tell the new kid. "It will stop hurting eventually."

You almost can't beagle-proof a house. At least in regards to food. They get on tables. They surf the kitchen counters. I had one that could open a refrigerator. My garbage is inside a kitchen closet, on top of a high shelf, with a super duper lid. Beagles see garbage as food. You learn that the hard way when you take a small nap on the couch in the evening and wake up to a kitchen floor that looks like a college kid's apartment on Saturday morning— pizza crust strewn everywhere, knocked over trash can, and copious quantities of spilled containers. Some experts say beagles are stupid. They are not. But they have NO impulse control. The same stubborn tenacity that lets a beagle chase a rabbit till it is shot will also allow the same hound to steal food and tear into the garbage, even though it knows it will be punished.

Beagles are cute. You can start with every intention of not allowing your adorable house hound to get on the furniture. It won't be long until your legs ache because the dogs sleep while leaning against your body, preventing you from moving your legs all night long. You don't realize how much you move in your sleep, until you can't do it. A 13" beagle takes up more bed space than my wife, who claims to be five feet and four inches tall. That depends, I think, on the hairstyle. A sleeping 15" beagle can occupy more space than a compact car. An "official 15" beagle" (Which is more like 23 ½" tall in some circles, and looks like a walker coon hound, requires you to buy a king sized bed). And then you sleep on the couch.

I buy lint rollers by the gross. The same experts that call beagles stupid also say that beagles do not shed. Trust me, they do. Couches, shirts, pants, car seats, and everything you own will require that you buy a good vacuum cleaner and a fantastic dog brush. When I empty my lint tray from the clothes dryer, it looks like somebody skinned a dozen deer. I keep duct tape in my truck just to remove the hair on my clothes that were not quite visible when I was inside. The modern energy efficient lights do not seem to illuminate a house as well as the old bulbs.

There are advantages. I find that house beagles handle better. They listen to me and seem to hunt closer to me. Don't get me wrong, I cannot call my dog off a screaming hot chase, but they will handle in the field while they are searching for a rabbit. There are lots of fantastic dogs that never learned their names until they were quite old, since they were started on rabbits and never really given much attention until they were deemed to be "keepers." Go to a trial and you will see dogs that are almost unable to be caught. So "Tally-Ho" also replaces "Down" and "Here" so that the dogs can be leashed.

House dogs are great for letting you know when someone is coming to your house. Sure, this seems obvious. No doubt there are fantastic advantages in that the dogs are good for keeping you aware of burglars and criminals. The real advantage, however, is that you can be notified when your wife is coming home. Drinking milk out of the carton? Dog will let you know that you better stop. Promise to take the garbage out before she left and it is still in the house (inside the closet, remember)? No problem, just spring to your feet and haul it out the back door as she comes in the front. Got some project on the kitchen table that is causing knife marks to mar the surface? One bark and you know that you have one minute for her to get to the door from the driveway. This is an invaluable benefit to having beagles in the house.

Beagles are also good for culinary purposes. Chunk of bread get rock hard? Beagles can help. Burn the roast a little on the outside? That's extra protein in the hard running season. Did your wife make some meal you do not like? Fido eats garbage, remember? He will certainly eat the gourmet thing. Ever have a friend give you leftovers from a social function, and they are simply not good? Beagle is there to the rescue. I get doggie bags in restaurants all the time—and the stuff is for the dog.

The best part, however, is that the beasts are pleasant pets. They can brighten up your day. A faithful hound can lift your spirits after a bad day at work. You will never oversleep a day in your life! House beagles exude a calmness that embodies tranquility, at least until the doorbell rings or a potato chip bag is moved. Just keep in mind that the money you save in building a kennel will be spent locking your garbage and refrigerator and cabinets!

"ONE...TWO..."

Parenting has changed directions in recent decades for sure. Many people that train dogs will tell you that if a hound is given treats for doing what it is supposed to do, then the owner of the dog is actually being trained to give the dogs treats. The same seems true with kids insofar as the current parenting strategy seems to be that kids are given rewards for doing good things, and the hope is that they will simply cease to do bad things as they are in perpetual pursuit of rewards. Once a dog's appetite is sated (it can technically happen to a beagle), it may well refuse to obey commands. Surely we have all seen kids, sitting amidst more toys than they even knew they owned, refuse to do a task assigned by one of their parents. I saw this recently in a grocery store where a kid was in a showdown with Mom. I am not sure what precipitated the argument, as I arrived in the checkout line after the debate had evolved into spectacle.

"Please?" Mom hissed through her teeth without opening here mouth. Mom's all think that if they pretend to be a ventriloquist then no one will recognize that it is her kid that is being problematic.

"No!" the little boy shouted at the top of his lungs.

"I told you I would buy you a toy!" Mom retaliated. Not only was her mouth moving but she was waving her arms frantically. She had ceased to care if anyone knew that her kid was being problematic.

"I don't want a toy!"

I could tell right away that this kid was reared in the modern notion that rewards are necessary to properly raise a child. He obviously had more toys than he wanted, and the stakes had to be raised.

"Fine!" Mom was not only moving her lips and waving her arms, but she began to spit her words in such a way that her pony tail, which I had just then noticed was frazzled and bursting at the rubber-band-thing that contained it, was swaying and bobbing as she yelled, "I will buy you the battery powered toy jeep if you be quiet and behave until we get home."

Quid pro quo is always won by a kid when there is no punishment.

No one whose entire childhood was in the last century ever felt that they lacked toys. We only got toys on rare instances. Many of my toys were sticks from the woods, or salvaged materials. My Captain America costume consisted of a garbage can lid that was found in the yard after a powerful wind storm. I spray painted it the appropriate red, white, and blue with paint that I got from a garage in the neighborhood that had a few cans of paint that were not quite empty. Later we determined that it belonged to the neighbors, and my wonderful shield was yet again a garbage can lid. We never did get anything good after any other wind storm—just a lawn chair and a bunch of leaves. Well, once I found a small, plastic swimming pool of the sort made for little kids, but it was mangled beyond belief in the journey to our neighborhood. I never could seal all the holes in the pool to my satisfaction. My plan was to raise minnows in there and sell them to fisherman. Mom ended that dream of entering the bait fish business.

"Get rid of it," she said. That was all. She had a wooden spoon and she wasn't afraid to use it. Parent's routinely use "time-outs" in an attempt to discipline kids now. I would have loved to have an option to go sit by myself as punishment. "Jimmy," I once heard a mom say to her kid, "If you don't rinse the dirty plates from supper and put them in the dishwasher you are going to get a time-out." The kid promptly refused to do the chore and had to sit quietly on a chair while his mother did the dishes. The kid was brilliant. My mother never really had a time-out system. It was more of a countdown. She would count to three, and then if I was not moving with a great deal of enthusiasm and earnest she would whack me with the spoon. It was a long-handled wooden spoon. It was the same one she used to stir the Kool-Aid, and I would sometimes get a little nervous when she grabbed it to mix up a new container of the stuff. She only counted to three, and with few exceptions it was a fast count. Sometimes she started running at me before she even got to three. In other words, there were few rewards used to motivate kids then and a lot of punishment. It wasn't all wooden spoons— sometimes it was just a refusal to let you go play outside or maybe not providing a ride to a friend's house.

"Keep it up and I will tell your father when he gets home," was a common threat. Have you ever heard of good parent/bad parent? It is where one parent is the nice one and the other is the enforcer. My parents played mean parent/meaner parent. Basically, if Mom felt that you were not sufficiently disciplined with her actions she would threaten to tell Father. Kids lived under the impression that their own mischief could put a man in a terrible mood. We never thought that the jobs our fathers worked could be the source of their unhappiness, as they walked into the house tired, dirty, and sweaty. Probably because at that age all little boys thought being covered in mud and sweat was the sign of a fantastic bicycle ride!

But moms and dads were also the source of the good things. When I got beagles as a kid, I really wanted to have a nice hunting vest. I had a hunting coat, but that was not the same, especially in the hotter days of the early hunting season. I managed to come by a nice hunting vest at a yard sale. It was used and a little big, but it was just what I needed. My only problem was that it had no orange. My home state of Pennsylvania required blaze orange to be worn on the head, chest and back. The vest was obviously from an older era, before blaze orange, though it was in great condition. Mom sewed orange fabric onto the vest to make it legal. She paid more for the fabric than I did for the vest.

She also was great about whoppers. What I mean by that is she would lie to the school. I was allowed to skip in order to go hunting or fishing. Don't get me wrong, it wasn't all that often, and it had to be on a day when I had no tests scheduled. I loved those events though. She also fibbed about appointments. In the early fall, during the weeks that dad worked 11-7, he would get out of work at 7 a.m. and be home 15 minutes later. I would be ready to rabbit hunt when he got home. We would shoot a couple rabbits and then come home. I would make it to school with an excuse in my pocket from my mother stipulating that I had an appointment with the dentist or optometrist. I wore glasses, so they were always in need of replacement or repair. Those days were not counted as absences—I had to go to the doctor for just part of the day!

One of the things that I remember particularly well is the berry quotas. Mom and Gram were big proponents of picking berries for jelly. They would give my sister and I a bucket and say, "Go fill it." It didn't matter what berry was in season either. We would go out the door and not return until the bucket was full. "You know," my sister said, "whenever we return too fast, they give us a bigger bucket the next day." Until that moment I hadn't realized how smart my younger sister was. So we decided that we could not return too quickly. I would take the beagles and look for rabbits. I would get some fantastic chases. Found great hunting spots.

I also learned what it sounds like when your dog heads out of the county chasing a deer or fox. Once I had the terrible experience of getting a dog stuck in brush so thick that I cut my whole body getting in there to remove the jagged stump from where it was stuck through his collar. When it was too hot to pick berries or even run dogs she would drive me to some pond to catch fish that she would fry for supper. At the time I was allergic to fish, so I would get something else, but I was just glad to go fishing!

I remember she once paid a very expensive veterinary bill for my first beagle as a puppy when he had parvovirus, and she paid a fairly hefty bill for that hound again when he had a porcupine encounter that could not be remedied with a pair of pliers. Not many years before she died I asked her about all these things.

"Oh," she waved her hand, "I never minded driving you to the woods or a fishing hole."

"Did it make you mad when the dogs had vet bills?" I asked

"No. Some boys in town had legal fines for getting in trouble." She sighed.

"What?" I asked.

"Oh, one of my friends told me that a mom can't pick her kids' friends," Mom said, "and I decided that she had to be wrong."

"Really," I asked.

"Yep. Her kid got in trouble at school and she said that bad friends can do that. But you can't pick those for your kids. Well, I decided then and there to keep my kids around the right influence. You just wanted to be in the woods with dogs anyway!"

"Ha!" I snorted.

"Whenever you were little and hanging out with a bad kid, I drove you and those dogs to the woods when your dad was working. When you were a teenager with a driver's license, I gave you the car to go hunting."

"You didn't trust me to pick friends?" I said.

"Nope," she said, "but give you a beagle and a chase and you forgot about bad things."

"I can't believe you!" I raised my voice just a little.

"Don't yell at me! One . . . two . . ." she started to count to three.

"Thanks, Mom," I said. And I meant it. And I mean it even more now that she is gone. Happy Mother's Day.

WHISTLE WHILE YOU PLAY

It is not at all uncommon for kids to make a big production over Father's Day. Dad gets his favorite meal and activities are centered upon his hobbies and interests. It doesn't seem that it was that way in my youth. We made a big deal about Mother's Day. We took *her* out to a restaurant, so that *she* would not have to cook that day. The food wasn't as good, but she didn't have to cook. We always had a dessert or ice cream or both. It was a family affair. Dad didn't get many days off work, and almost never on Sundays. So Father's day consisted of buying dad a tool for his second job of carpentry work—something newfangled that he may or may not use or perhaps a replacement tool for something he had worn out. The most important part of Father's Day was to leave Dad alone! Oh, I don't mean we had to hide, but depending on what shift he was working that day, he might be sleeping in the middle of the day, getting ready to go to the factory, or coming home and ready to relax.

The last thing he liked was to be confronted with a crisis when he walked in the door. This is why my mother's typical dose of punishment was simply looking and me and saying, "Do you want me to tell your father what you did when he gets home?" That statement alone was enough to send cold shivers through a kid, especially if dad was working 16-hour shifts that week. Of course Father's Day is in the summer, so the standard operating procedure was to send me and my sister outside to play. "Go to the playground and make all the noise you want," being the typical commandment. This is when kids played outside in packs. The packs were mostly divided along size and gender. Boys roamed around with boys their own age, and girls roamed around with girls their own age. When we became teenagers we combined packs, and the boys tried to impress the girls and the girls laughed at us. Turkey and deer and every other critter in the natural world have males make fools of themselves for female approval. The females tolerate this behavior and approve of the winners. Girls are smart—they let boys make fools of themselves, and even when the young lad thinks he has done something impressive the girl will be able to dismiss him as lacking good sense. The girls act like humans. Boys, for their part, continue to act like animals.

Another difference was that dads did not take an interest in kids' things. I overheard a father just the other day talking to his kid about her favorite cartoon. My dad did not know anything about Star Wars, Star Trek, or the video games at the arcade. Kids went to dark buildings with a pocket full of quarters to play video games then. Now they hack into their mom's Amazon account and have the games delivered to the door! Well, my stepson does. This isn't to say that my dad was offended by the things I did; he just wasn't going to do any homework to learn about them. "Hey, Dad," I once said, "the new Star Wars Movie is coming out, and Han Solo is frozen and Luke Skywalker had his hand cut off. What do you think will happen in the next movie?"

"Speaking of frozen," he said, "you left the ice cube tray on the counter and it melted. Your mom ain't happy. Just so you know." He was not going to watch those movies to talk with me about them. I called my buddy Lenny the other day, "What are you doing?" I asked.

"Watching some stupid cartoon about guppies," he said.

"Why?" I asked.

"Cuz it is all my granddaughter talks about, and my wife said I have to learn about it so I can hold a discussion with her." He was doing homework. My dad would not have been so involved in those kinds of things. School grades and activities were something he cared about. He would help his kids in sports. If I enjoyed the same interests as Dad, I could tag along. This was great for hunting and fishing. Fishing was the first outdoor pursuit that I was allowed to do, as there is no minimum age to participate. I have to confess that I was more thrilled about crawling as a kid than I am now. I mention that because the tranquil image of a fly fisherman standing in waist high water on a broad stream is a myth. Well, it is rare anyway, at least where I grew up. Our trout streams are covered with low hanging trees and underbrush, forcing you to low crawl to the water where you then cast. By cast, I mean tie a live minnow to your fly rod and let the line drift downstream. This is hard enough to accomplish by yourself, let alone with a child in close proximity that has never caught a fish and desperately wants to do so. Dad was very patient with me while we shared cramped space, fumbling with a live minnow jig. Naturally, I wanted to bait my own fly rod (I know that statement just sent some fishing purists into apoplexy), and I ended up with barely live minnows by the time I got them jigged. Sometimes we used salted minnows instead. Obviously I insisted on taking every piece of fishing gear I had accumulated from my various sources with us on every single fishing trip.

Most of my sources were streams where I would watch somebody lose a hook or lure, and I would wade into the water after they left to try and get it. I also had tackle that people would give me, mostly stuff that never caught a fish. A neighbor with a boat gave me a bunch of lures for ocean and lake fishing. I had a few sinkers that could be boat anchors for a canoe. I drug all of this gear with me at any fishing trip, much to my dad's dismay. My tackle box was almost the size of a hope chest, and twice as heavy.

Hunting came when I was 12, and this was much more to my liking. Reading magazines made me want a dog in the worst way, and a neighbor kid had a beagle. I begged for a beagle and was able to talk dad into getting one when I was 13. I didn't know it then, but my father had owned beagles in the 1940s and 1950s, and he had really enjoyed rabbit and hare hunting. He explained this shortly after I got my dog. He had gotten out of beagling due to a death. His favorite hunting dog was named Prince, and he was a descendent of Grey's Linesman, a famous beagle at the time. Prince had gone missing (escaped from the yard), and Dad did not worry, as he lived at the end of town and the dog would wander home after exhausting itself chasing rabbits. The dog went missing, and he searched for several days before being told that the dog was last seen hunting with my father's older brother. The two had disagreements going back to childhood, and Prince was found dead, shot in a field where the dog often found a rabbit. Not only did my uncle never admit to shooting the dog (by accident if he did, perhaps) but he also denied having been hunting with Prince, despite the testimony of a couple guys that saw him.

I wasn't born until 1972, and it had been nearly two decades since my father had owned a dog. He seemed reluctant at first, but we bought two dogs—I bought one, and he bought a half littermate. He named the bitch he bought Princess. From 1985 until 1991, when my dad died from cancer at the age of 64, we were perpetual partners in the field. Oh, and there was no sitting on the tailgate! We ran to get in front of the dogs and see how they were doing. We could not keep up with them, so we had to cut the diameter of the circles the rabbits were running to get ahead of them and try to see some hound work! It was a routine that was absolutely predictable. We either went to the woods at dawn or dusk in the summer—depending upon the shift he was working—and we ran the dogs. During the school year, we ran in the evening every day that he wasn't working the 3-11 shift. If it was hunting season, he would pick me up at school with the dogs and guns when the final bell rang and we would hunt until the legal shooting hours had expired.

"I'm glad you were so stubborn about wanting a dog," he said one day as Duke and Princess were pounding a rabbit and sending it in big, squared off circles, "I didn't think I could want another dog after I lost Prince all those years ago."

"This is fun," I said as the hounds blasted by. We would run to another opening to see the rabbit go by us again. I can still see his tall and lean frame sprinting through the underbrush. He was a very fast runner too. I remember how he whistled for the dogs. When they were not chasing a rabbit, but were far away trying to find one, he would whistle. It was the loud whistle that you can only make by putting your fingers in your mouth.

"How do you do that?" I asked in frustration.

"Put your middle finger from each hand on your tongue's tip, push your tongue in, and force air out of your lungs as hard as you can. I desperately wanted to be able

64

to do that. He could call the dogs from phenomenal distances. He trained them to come to this whistle as pups, giving them a bit of a hotdog when they obeyed. I practiced this whistle for two days, for sessions that lasted hours (until I got a headache) and taking a break to recover. Suddenly, it happened—a loud piercing whistle. I was so thrilled! I too could call dogs the same way. So often, when I am at field trials, I see guys that can't even call their dogs when they are close by. They yell "Tally-ho" trying to trick the dog into believing that a rabbit has been located. Or they bark like a dog and run, imitating a dog chasing a rabbit in the hope that the dog will hark in to the "chase" that is not happening. I still teach pups to come to that loud whistle with hotdogs, and I can call them from a long distance. I have a tracking collar, but that whistle brings the dogs at a full charge, so long as they are not chasing a rabbit and can hear me.

Last year, in hunting season, I was with some fellows and called my dogs back in the same manner. A young hunter was with us, and he marveled at this call the same as I had done at his age. I showed him how to do it and said that he shouldn't be surprised if it takes him a couple days to learn how to do the same. Every time I call dogs I think of the first time I saw my father do it. I think it works better than any dog whistle and carries further than anything other than a hunting horn. Whether hunting, conditioning hounds, field trialing, or just running dogs with the gang, I am reminded of Dad every time I call the dogs back to me. Happy Father's Day.

Gundog Brace: More Gundog, or More Brace?

Many years ago I was at a Gundog Brace trial with a dog that sustained an injury. The injury was induced by a competitor as she swinging a plastic stick with full vigor against the brush in an attempt to find a rabbit. She attacked the vegetation with such ferocity that I thought perhaps there was a wild beast in there that must be kept at bay, or that it may even have locked her leg in its jaws. The dog that she had entered in the trial was walking casually along the mowed paths, patiently waiting for his master to find a rabbit. I know this because I too was walking along the mowed path, and then I heard a thud, followed by a yip, and then a gurgling noise. My dog was in the brush, looking for a rabbit, and she had hit him with the stick. He rolled over, and I was convinced he was dying.

"What the heck are you doing?!!" I yelled. Only I didn't say heck. I used a geographic reference to a place sometimes mentioned in the Bible. I ran over and knelt before my hound. The emotions of panic and anger mixed themselves together in my stomach producing angst.

"I was trying to find a rabbit!" she yelled, non-apologetically. In fact, she was hostile and upset that I had the nerve to be angry about her actions. "How was I supposed to know your dog was in that brush?!"

"Because we are at a Gundog Brace trial where dogs are scored in part on the ability to find a rabbit," I said without looking at her, my full attention on my dog.

"He should look out where he goes!"

At this point I am glad that the person talking to me was a woman and not a man, as I may not have lost just my temper but my eternal salvation as well due to a fist fight that went too far! Well, I would have been tempted to do such a thing anyway.

A few minutes later, my dog staggered to his feet with glazed eyes and stumbled away. He did not have a good chase, but he did heal fine. I think he may have been lucky to get hit in the head, where a cut was located, rather than his spine which may have broken under the blow. That was the day that I realized not all Gundog Brace trials are the same. There are things to indicate what you have stumbled into if you show up at a club parking lot.

One thing is armor. By armor I mean guys wearing tons of fabric that protects the wearer from briars. If you see lots of guys wearing thorn proof bibs and coats, that can be a clue that you are at a trial that is more brace than gundog. Sure, the judges and field marshal may need such clothes. At beagle clubs, I always wear brush pants when running dogs, but full body briar armor is an indicator that the dogs won't be finding the rabbits. Which leads me to my next sure sign that you may have driven to the wrong trial . . .

"Tally-Ho" sticks are what you call the thing that knocked my dog unconscious all those years ago. They come in many forms. I have seen some that are golf clubs with the heads sawed off in order to produce a lightweight metallic stick. Fiberglass is a common modern form. I have seen ski poles customized in such a way that it brings about the desired velocity that generates a whistling sound as it cleaves through the air and removes the top of weeds. Very often these trials will arrange a gallery of guys in skirmish lines that march through the brush like Redcoats taking the battlefield against the Continental militia while brandishing these tally-ho sticks. This march stampedes chipmunks, songbirds, and rabbits onto paths where they can be witnessed by other people that are called "spotters." The marching soldiers sound like a combination of cracking whips and helicopter rotors as they methodically push into the brush, staying in formation.

Spotters are often a little older, and they have replaced their tally-ho sticks with a shorter stick that has a handle that unfolds into a seat. Honest, I am not making this up.

They stab the stick into the ground, unfold the seat, and lean on it while they stay on a grassy path and watch for a rabbit emerge. If the Redcoats arrive and no rabbit has preceded them, then the guy with the stick-chair moves ahead of the next block of brush and the process is repeated. Blocks of brush, by the way, are another good sign that you may have gone to the wrong place. When the brushy cover is characterized by many parallel paths, sometimes consuming 40 percent of the total area of the running grounds, then you know the club may have this mentality that is more brace than gundog.

"Tally-Ho" will be shouted with great vigor, as if the last rabbit on earth has been spotted. If your dog does not know that word, then you will be viewed with great suspicion at a club that is more brace than gundog. In fact, I once saw a guy corrected for yelling "Tally" rather than the entire "Tally-Ho." It was seen as a serious breach of etiquette. In fact, the last time I saw such scornful looks heaped upon a person was when I attended a dinner that had lots of forks and I started with the wrong one, and when I chose to use a small spoon for my soup. My wife was quite embarrassed at my behavior. I used the same fork for the entire meal.

Please understand that I do like the brace format, as it allows ample opportunity to see the hounds. But some clubs will slow the dogs down and will look for style over accomplishment. They do not want the dogs to run too fast or go over the end of the scent trail even a few feet when the rabbit has changed direction. I once saw a judge order the brace to be handled when my dog got a sight chase "Handle them before the rabbit is caught!" he screamed.

"Catching the rabbit makes you high brace, right?" His cheeks quivered and his left eye developed a rapid blinking condition. He gave me a sympathetic look like you might give to a little kid that was trying very hard to ride a bicycle and has not yet learned the skill—poor kid might learn someday. The judge hoped that I might learn one or two things about beagles—eventually.

I hate to be the guy that keeps saying this, but the list of desired traits in the rulebook apply to all formats— brace, small pack option, or large pack. The same is true for the faults that are listed and defined. You just have to ask yourself if a gundog brace event is more gundog or more brace. Oh, and I do often walk with a hiking stick when running my dogs. But it is all wood and used primarily for walking down hill on wet grass with rubber boots in order to keep me from falling when my feet slip. And I have never hit a dog with it.

A Long Leash

I can honestly say that my father did more for me than I ever knew at the time. Modern fathers are hyper-involved with every detail of their children's lives. They schedule play dates with the neighbors' kids, carry infants in back packs, and drive them everywhere. You had to be old enough to run to go places with my dad—he wasn't carrying his kids, and he was going to walk at a normal stride, which forced a small kid to run in order to keep up. He didn't really take us in the vehicle to a friend's house either. We were given bicycles, and we could go anywhere that we could get on those things without crossing busy roads, which were forbidden. We covered vast distances riding down railroad tracks and logging roads. We pedaled to fishing holes, ball games, and berry patches. This, of course, was back in the 1900s when no one worried too much about kids wandering around in packs without adult supervision. In the summer we had to be home at five o'clock for supper, and no one really looked for us until then. Actually, closer to 5:30 before they got worried. The fire hall sounded an air raid siren at five that could be heard for miles. Gangs of kids scattered at the sound to make it home before being declared late for supper. We'd stumble in the door, drenched in sweat from the mad dash home from wherever we happened to be at the time.

If we were late, then some concern would creep into our parents. There would be worry if something did happen— an accident or a busted bicycle chain could really make a kid late. More often than not, however, the kid came home just fine and the concern was instantly transformed to wrath, "Are you trying to make us worry? What is wrong with you?!" Such scolding was the reason that we all set land speed records getting home when the air raid siren sounded.

Dad also never imposed a curfew if I was in the woods. Going to town was another matter, but he let me roam the hills. When we were teenagers, we began to take camping more seriously as an attempt to find deer hunting spots. I should explain. In the 1900s people had to go out in the woods and look for deer tracks, deer scrapes, and buck rubs. Digital cameras had not yet been invented, and thus they could not be strapped to trees so that people could determine where the big deer live. The only camera we had spit out the picture and required the photographer to shake it vigorously while the photographic film "developed" before your very eyes. It took forever to get a good picture at a large family gathering—someone had blinked, or some person had red eyes, or somebody felt that she looked fat and wanted to do it all over again! Sorry, I digressed. We had no trail cams then. We would camp in the woods, sit on deer trails at dusk, and wake up early to look for sign again in the morning.

"Dad," I said, "we are going to go camping tonight and look for some deer hunting spots for fall. Is that okay with you?"

"Sure," he said without looking up from the newspaper. Suddenly he dropped his paper and fixed his gaze on me. "How old are you?"

"Sixteen. That's why I am looking. I can hunt alone now."

"Yeah, whatever. You are looking for deer?" he stared into my soul.

"Yes."

"You guys aren't paying some loser to buy beer for yinz are you?" He kept staring.

"No," I confessed honestly.

"You don't have a bunch of girls telling lies to their parents about a sleepover and meeting you out there in the woods, do you?" He was folding the newspaper at that point.

"No," I gulped.

"Okay. Go ahead."

Later that day I talked to the guys. "What did your dad say about camping?" a friend asked.

"He said I could go. And he had a couple of really good ideas!" I explained. None of us knew that many girls.

Fortunately we didn't know anyone old enough to buy beer either. In retrospect I can see how my dad had learned a lot of things from having four sons and daughter before me. They were all raised and had kids my age or older. I am guessing that there must have been a camping trip gone awry at some point in his earlier parenting days, as evidenced by his questions.

I am most thankful for sharing beagles with my dad. We spent countless hours together watching the dogs chase and listening to hound music echo off the hills. There are so many sports that people tend to do only in their youth—baseball, for instance. I haven't played baseball since I was a kid. Football is another sport that we can only do as kids, unless you are one of the fortunate few to play in college. As you read this, I have been chasing beagles through the woods for thirty years this month, a life-long sport! My dad has been dead since 1991, but I can still remember the time we spent afield like it was yesterday. I can imagine his voice saying, "Why do you need a satellite to find your dogs?" or "Does it feel better to miss with an expensive shotgun?" or "Why do you have those dogs in your house?"

No, there are many things my dad taught me. He let me ruin a good pocket knife learning how to sharpen it with a whetstone. He showed me how to track a deer, shoot rifles and shotguns, catch trout, start a fire with one match, and to respect the outdoors. He taught me to face my fears, and when I was playing baseball as a youngster and was afraid of the ball when thrown by the faster pitchers, he took me out for batting practice and hit me with the ball a dozen or so times to get me over the fear. He taught me to drive a two-wheel drive truck in the muddiest and snowiest conditions, and I still feel spoiled to own a four-wheel drive truck.

But it is this life gone to the dogs that I am most thankful to have received from Dad. What a joyous gift. Sometimes, when the early morning fog is socked into the hills and my beagles chase without my seeing them I can almost hear the dogs that he and I owned together. I can smell his pipe and hear his satisfied laughter as a dog solves a tough check where the rabbit has doubled back on its own tracks.

I still take great satisfaction at shooting a limit of rabbits and only dirtying one barrel of my side by side. Dad always thought that was the sign of a good shooter. I still like 16 gauge shotguns, I think because my father preferred them. I like leather leashes. When I was a kid we got them from Blett Dog Supply in Sunbury, Pennsylvania. French snaps—the good ones, which are actually made in Germany. I like an O ring on the end of the lead that goes over the hand, so that the snap can be attached to it, forming a closed circuit that can be worn diagonally across my torso, with the leash resting across my left shoulder.

I still prefer leather leashes, and I still wear them the same way. I order them longer than standard so that they hang to my beltline. I think that is more comfortable, but over the years I have decided that comfort has nothing to do with the reason I prefer a leash that can be snapped to itself, in order to form a loop that hangs to my beltline. No, I think I prefer these long leads because they fall across my body as they did when I was thirteen years old, when I had my first beagle.

If you will excuse me, there is a forecast for morning fog. I want to get ready to leave early for the beagle club. I have one dog that sounds a lot like a beagle my dad had when I was a kid. If the dew drenched grass gets my rubber boots wet, and if the fog floats so as to shroud the topography in such a way that it could be anywhere, then the same elements may give the landscape the appearance of being in "anytime."

When that happens I find myself in a state where my Duke's voice could well be Princess in 1985 and the West Branch Beagle Club might well be the running grounds of my youth. I won't be able to see my truck through the ground clouds, so it may well be a 1977 two-wheel drive Ford pickup. I won't spoil the moment by looking at my GPS. Happy Father's Day.

CLUBBING

For reasons that make no sense to my wife, I have always loved camping. I can get her to go along sometimes, but there are other instances when she seems to think that this is sort of a waste of time. I have always enjoyed camping. "What is it with you?" my wife asks. "You get sleepy and head to the woods like most people go to a bedroom." I have to confess, that it does seem odd. I think it started when I was a kid. Air conditioning is fairly commonplace now, but when I was a youngster we had one air conditioner, and it was a window unit that lived in my parents' bedroom.

Dad changed shifts every week, and this meant that there were weeks in the summer when he would be sleeping in the middle of the afternoon so that he could go to work at 11 o'clock that night. It would get to be over 80 degrees in the upstairs of the house in the summer and the air was stifling. It would often cool down in the evening, but not always. Sometimes opening the window helped, but other times it just allowed humid air to enter the house and make your perspiration cling to your skin and drip rather than instantly evaporate.

The air conditioner never resided in the window all year. That would be crazy as it would allow frigid air to rush into the house during the winter, cold winds pouring around and through the air conditioner. Dad seemed to stoke the wood burner until the house was anywhere between 80-90 degrees in the winter. There was no thermostat, you understand. At least not on a wall. There was one on the wood burner, and when it reached the prescribed setting, a fan would start and blow hot air through the labyrinth of ductwork he had running through the ceiling of the basement. Those ducts then emerged into rooms in the downstairs of our house or a couple went upstairs by travelling through closets to reach the second

74

floor of our home. The temperature of the furnace controlled the frequency of the fan's output of the hot air. It kept the furnace from overheating. The thermostat on our wall had once been utilized to control a natural gas furnace. In the late 1970s and early 80s, the cost of that fuel skyrocketed and dad got rid of the furnace and installed a wood burner in the basement. The thermostat on the wall then had no function, other than to tell you how hot or cold it was in the room. It was a glorified thermometer. There was no way to know what to expect when coming home from school and entering the house. It might be chilly, slightly cool, comfortable, warm, or volcanic.

The winter temperature, of course, all depended on the fire. Did it go out? Was it fed lots of wood? How was the outside temperature? The colder the weather the better the furnace burned, and the hotter it got inside. The furnace had a damper, and the damper setting dominated much of my father's winter time thoughts. At any rate, 80 degrees in the summer is comfortable where the same temperature in the winter seems intolerable! Dad was the guy that had to sleep in the afternoon sun, so the air conditioner was in his room. A fan was utilized to blow that cool air into the rest of the upstairs, meaning my sister's bedroom. My bedroom was too far away from the master bedroom to receive any relief. Actually, it was more of a closet. I am not kidding. I have been in modern homes with closets bigger than my bedroom. I had a small bed and a dresser drawer. I could stand and face the bed, or turn around and face the dresser. I once saw a documentary on life at sea, and they made a big deal about how small the sleeping quarters were on the boat. I would have been envious of that much space as a kid.

So I often went downstairs to sleep on the couch in the summer. But a tent seemed like a much better idea. You can put a tent on a hill in the summer and almost guarantee some breeze. After a sweaty day it was always nice to find some way to cool down. We would often go in the creek to cool down, but you couldn't sleep there. The wood burner meant that we had to have firewood, and from the age of 12 until I moved to college the task of splitting firewood was mine. I do not recall seeing a wood splitter in my youth of the sort commonly used by contemporary homeowners that opt to use firewood. There was no way of putting a log onto a machine and pulling the lever so that a crushing load of power forced the round of timber into perfect quarters of firewood. My dad had a different kind of wood splitter—an axe, wedges, and me. I even had a safety lesson. "Don't stand too close to the round you are splitting or you will hit the handle and that can break it." Dad puffed his pipe. "Then I have to go get a new handle. Stores don't open until eight o'clock in the morning, and I am usually going to work at seven or coming home at that hour. So this is a hassle. DON'T stand too close! Gauge your distance and split it." He whacked a piece in demonstration, sending split wood in all directions with one massive swing.

"Okay," I said, hitting a piece of wood squarely but not hard enough to split it cleanly on the first swing.

"You'll get the hang of it," Dad said. "Oh yeah, one more thing. If you stand too far away from the wood you will miss entirely and the axe will come straight down on you. So keep your feet spread apart or you will cut your foot off."

Did you notice that the axe handle seems to have received more concern than my feet? He also had a safety lesson on heat stress.

"I chain sawed those logs to the length of our wood burner. I'd suggest you start splitting them early in the morning before it gets hot each day. It has to all be split by the time the school year starts. August is hot, and you don't want to have to split it all then. You can get hurt if you overheat too much. Have a good summer break."

To this day when I visit cities and see makeshift cities of tents I have the same thought: "Probably a bunch of kids that lived in a home that burns wood for heat and they ran away." There were plenty of nights when sleeping in the woods, on top of a windy hill, inside of a tent, was the best possible way to get some sleep. I could walk straight up hill from my house and find my way to Gordon's farm. There were rabbits at Gordon's farm, and I was allowed to go anywhere on the property I wanted. I loved going down below the pastures and into the goldenrod to chase a woods rabbit. They were big running bunnies that gave large circles, often into taller timber. The dogs sometimes sounded like they were chasing a deer on those rabbits, but it was very rare for that to be the case. Farmers are good about keeping the deer to a minimum. It would have only taken a half hour to walk the dogs home when I was finished with my evening rabbit chase, but then I would have to walk back to my campsite. More importantly, I would have been in the woods alone, and I was always certain that there were bears, mountain lions, and wolves waiting to devour me.

No, I preferred to sleep with the two beagles in the tent with me. Two beagles on a summer night meant no sleeping bag! If I put my tent just barely off the farm, but on the ridge, I had a good flow of air all night. I packed just enough dog food and sandwiches wrapped in wax paper for me. I used the wax paper to start a campfire for light. The dogs drank from the creek and I brought a canteen full of water from home for me. In the morning I would let the dogs chase another rabbit before going home to split firewood.

The worst part of the camping trips was the bull. I never knew for sure where the Gordon bull would be. If you have been around farms then you know that some bulls are very aggressive and others are demonic. The Gordon bull was the latter. I initially felt that I should try and leash my dogs and lead them to safety with me. Stopping to bend over and leash a dog is never a good idea in the presence of a bull. So I began walking close to the edges of pastures, giving myself the opportunity to dive through, over, or under a barbed wire fence (depending on the topography of the fence line at any given point) in order to avoid the horns. Massively deep cuts are never fun. But I chose the barbed wire anyway! Getting stomped and hooked by a bull was never a good idea to me. Sometimes I could stop at the Gordon farm and ask them where the bull was pastured. The problem with farmers is that they are never home. Well, they are home, but not in the house. There is too much work to be done so you have to search for them in barns, fields, garages, and any number of places where they might have to go in order to get parts to repair their equipment.

Finding a farmer always meant that they were behind, since they were standing still enabling you to locate them. They were repairing something, or waiting for a delivery, or doing something that enabled you to find them in the first place. I never wanted to bother anyone cutting hay. Some farmers will put you to work if you find them. "Sure you can hunt rabbits. Do you mind helping me load a few bales of hay first?" "Few" is a relative term. I actually like farm work in moderation, and I like to help out a little. I did sometimes find Hazel at the house. "Hey, I am going camping. Can you tell me where the bull is?"

"Yep, he's in one of those pastures. Hmm. Now where did Claude leave him last? Sit down and have a piece of pie. Maybe he will return in the meantime."

At any rate, there was the occasional frenzied escape from the bull. It wasn't every day or even every week, but it happened enough to keep me on my toes and walking the perimeter of the fence line. I loved those trips. Cool night air blowing through my tent and two slumbering beagles at my feet. I wouldn't trade those days for anything.

I have an air conditioner in my bedroom now. And there were many Fridays that I would drive to our beagle club to run rabbits after supper in these hot summer months, drive home, sleep in the air conditioning, and then return to the club the next morning. I started calculating the gasoline expense and decided I might be better off camping at the club! An ideal Friday night is spent listening to hound music until after dark, a campfire, and good night's sleep with a whippoorwill alarm system to start chasing rabbits again just before dawn. I live in a college town; and you often heart r guys talking about going out to the clubs with their friends. If I say me and the boys are going clubbing, that means that I am taking my three youngest male beagles to the beagle club for the night. And when I start to drift off to sleep in my rooftop tent, I am flooded with memories of childhood beagle camping. The dogs sleep under me now, in their dog box, and I still like having them close to wake me when critters approach. Sometimes I wake up looking for a bull.

CONDITIONED

We are getting into the hottest part of the year, and I for one do not like it. My dogs do not like it either. I have always been one to sing the praises of the beagle as the complete companion dog—great in the field and pleasant in the house. I really think that if you do not have a beagle in the house you are really missing out on part of what makes this breed so special. I have convinced a few people to do the same and move their hunting dogs in the house. Many of them have written me with words such as, "Ford, you're an idiot," or "It is cheaper to build a kennel than to fix a house so that the beagle won't steal people food or get into the garbage," and "Your wife knows you're an idiot, right?"

I only shared the pleasant messages I have received. The harsh ones I will keep to myself. Suffice it to say, there are some difficulties in housebreaking. You cannot leave a beagle pup have free roam of the house. You have to be with the beast when he is out and playing, not napping on the couch while the puppy rambles. The same stubborn tenacity that will let that youngster chase a rabbit until it is shot or goes in a hole can become the same tenacity that allows the pup to squat and relieve herself on your floor. Crate training is essential. You are a warden for those first few months!

The most common myth I hear is that they can't hunt or handle the snow if they live in the house. This is not true at all, and I must sing the praises of a house beagle in terms of handling. They really do seem to obey commands in the field better for me. Snow has never been a problem for me until this past winter, and that was due to the severity of the temperatures and the ice. There were plenty of "outside" dogs that had the same troubles this year. Oh, and my biggest problem wasn't the paws but rather sores from the icy snow rubbing the males scrotums. This happens with sled dogs all the time. But I will tell you what has been problematic for me: air conditioning.

I like to come home and not be in 90-degree temperatures with high humidity. A little relaxation in the evening is fine for me. My dogs like to lie under the air conditioners too, and stretch out for a snooze. My dogs are in shape, and can run all day. They are muscled! But they can have what I call a "bad radiator." They get hot faster than other dogs that live outside; and I think it is due to the air conditioner. They can only go a couple hours in the heat.

"Boy, that dog looks good but evidently he is not conditioned," a friend of mine said. Duke was standing there panting and looking like he would prefer for me to pick him up and take him to the truck. I was worried he might spin in a circle three times and lay down to build a nest—extreme quitting by rulebook standards. The temperature was in the 80s, and my other dog was panting pretty hard too. My friend's dogs were panting hard, don't get me wrong, but they did not look as tired as mine!

"He looks out of condition," I said, "but that is because he is air conditioned! He is actually in good physical condition." This was not the first time I had seen my dogs more affected by soaring temperatures than other dogs. There are weeks in the summer I do not even run rabbits! I am not a big fan of night running, and I have made that abundantly clear to my friends. But in the summer there is little choice. Although to be honest I tend to run about four o'clock in the morning and run until the sun burns off the dew and the dogs get tired. I would rather cast the hounds in the dark and pick them up in the daylight. Also, I am more of a morning person, and I would rather wake up early than be driving home at midnight.

I call this a bad radiator when it happens to my dogs. When I graduated college, a friend of mine had a junky Dodge Omni. It had a bad radiator. Actually it had a bad fan, which caused it to overheat. He moved me to Seminary (yes, everything I owned fit in a Dodge Omni. Google it if you are a youngster too young to recall this hatchback) and it took 6 hours to get there. Whenever the temperature gauge started to climb, he would have to get out in the left lane and get fresh air blowing over the engine, which angered the real cars that were trying to go quickly in that lane. When it cooled off, he would tuck back into traffic.

My veterinarian and I are friends (I think I have paid for at least one year of college for her kids), and we text each other when I have hound health questions. I ran this theory, that air conditioning causes my dogs to tire faster in the summer past her while she was at a veterinarians' convention at Cornell University, perhaps the best veterinarian college in the country. She had been talking to someone earlier that day, and some sled dogs (never thought I would mention sled dogs twice in one article) in Alaska overheated on a flight where the temperature was 40 degrees Fahrenheit in the plane's cargo area. It felt hot, though, to the dogs that sleep on the tundra! Indeed, the ability to dissipate heat does seem to be related to what the animal considers to be its baseline. That temperature is about 70 degrees in my house. If it gets to 68, I do not complain. During a heat snap recently, I did not turn on the air conditioners. My wife returned to an 80-degree house and asked, "Why are you sitting there sweating?"

"I am training dogs," I answered.

"Are you suffering from heat stroke?" she wiped sweat from her forehead and turned on the window unit air conditioner. "You aren't training dogs. You are in the house."

"I was trying to keep the dogs from getting fatigued so quickly in the summer sun," I said. "I just need to get them to reset their natural thermostat to a hotter setting."

"When were you going to turn on the air conditioner?" she asked. I hadn't considered that yet, and as I was forming an answer in my head she gave me some words that were not nearly as pleasant and complimentary as the ones I had quoted from my readers about bringing beagles in the house. I had a dog get real hot in winners' pack when the dogs managed to hole a rabbit, or at least they were given credit for holing it and were asked to get a new rabbit. I was at Indiana County where the grounds are pretty swampy in places. That was fortunate, as I worked him into the soggy stuff to cool him down and get a drink when we were ordered to get another rabbit. Other dogs were not as hot as he was.

I considered, briefly, the possibility of having the dogs outside in the summer months to prevent this problem. I was thinking about it just recently, while patting my dog on the head as we sat on the couch in the air conditioned living room. The dog started to wiggle his paws and make little barking sounds as he reran that chase he had for an hour that morning when the temperatures were at their lowest. I love those little moments with house beagles. I then decided that I would just not worry about these hot months and would be more than pleased to stay out of the hot sun myself! Come autumn it will be clear that my dogs have plenty of endurance in the cooler temperatures. May they come soon!

BURGERS AND ICE

You will have to bear with me, but I have an odd personality trait. My wife, Renee, says that there are an extreme amount of odd traits in my personality, but she doesn't know everything. I can prove this, because in the years we have been married there was one occasion when she told me I was correct on a disputed matter. I wrote it down on a calendar, and sometimes, when I get to feeling blue, I will dig out that calendar from 2007 and turn to the month of November. Granted, the dispute was over a rabbit hunting trip, but still I was correct that one day!

Anyway, the odd personality trait is this: I will not eat ice cream in the winter and I will not eat soup in the summer. My preference for summertime meals is actually breakfast cereal. It is just about perfect in the summer. Several years ago we planned on having some friends to the house to see the fireworks for the Fourth of July. State College has one of the biggest displays in the country, and the plan was to sit in the church parking lot on lawn chairs and watch it happen! Granted, the lower fireworks would not be visible, but everything else would be perfectly clear. And we would not have to fight traffic in the least. People routinely park ¼ mile away for the same view. A couple years ago, Renee decided to serve fancy pants pizza to everyone. The oven was in use for hours and all sorts of custom pizzas were being cooked. There were more topping choices than I can remember, but there were several fruits available as options, which seemed weird to me.

The worst part was entering the house after all the fireworks were over. We turned off the air conditioning because people were going in and out of the house so frequently, and the heat from the oven combined with the blasts of hot, outside air raised the house temperature into the high 80s! I know that the local news always cautions the public about the problem of the loud booms and bangs scaring dogs but quite honestly I have the opposite problem—my dogs get excited and think that they are missing the best rabbit hunt ever! I know what you are thinking: how could a dog mistake that much noise for a rabbit hunt? Well, first of all, I miss a lot. Second of all, they don't realize that I only ever miss twice (because I only have two shots in a double barrel) they just have come to associate loud booms with rabbit hunting and the occasional dead rabbit. I am still trying to teach them the difference between a rifle and a shotgun so that they do not get over excited when they see me grab the .30-06 to go deer hunting. There are limitations.

So the whole time our guests sat in the parking lot, our house beagles were in the fenced yard ricocheting and trying to hark into the fireworks display that they identified as a battery of shotguns up on the hill where they presumed they could fund dozens of guys that miss as many rabbits as I do. Even on years when I choose to not watch the fireworks and stay inside the house, I have the problem that my hounds are desperately trying to make it to the rabbit hunt and their excitement cannot be contained.

Last year we opted for a very different holiday. Andy Purnell and I went to our beagle club and ran dogs well into the night. My wife was there too, and Andy brought his neighbor Kenny to help handle hounds. Kenny is an adult that lives with his parents and mentally challenged; so Andy would always look after him to make sure he was okay. In fact, Andy did more to broaden Kenny's horizons and give him confidence than anyone. He gave Kenny ribbons from trials and would let Kenny have a dog or two to call his own. Kenny loved using the riding mower. Andy was always being generous to anyone in need. Anyway, I had pre-made hamburger patties to cook on the grill.

"Dude, what are those?" Andy looked into the cooler.

"Burgers," I answered as I lit the charcoal.

"They look like disk shaped meatloaves," he kept his eyes on the patties as he talked to me.

"You don't have to eat any," I said.

"Oh," he fixed his gaze on me, "I don't have a problem with those flat meatloaves."

They were half-pound burgers—75% beef and 25% pork. I had cooked and crumbled bacon mixed into the raw meat, as well as garlic powder, onion powder and a splash of A1 steak sauce. Cheese choices were Swiss, cheddar, or provolone. Kaiser rolls were required to hold the things, and condiments covered the gamut of mustards as well as mayonnaise, ketchup, lettuce, onion, tomato, and several peppers. Naturally, we had chips, sides and all the rest, including a nice campfire as we listened to the dogs run after the sun had set into the western sky.

We sat around and talked dogs. I was once in a philosophy class where there were long, seemingly pointless discussions on defining words like "being" or "essence." Indeed, sometimes philosophy can seem like a long debate over the definition of words. I think my wife became dreadfully bored as Andy and I talked about hunt, desire, and foot as it pertains to beagles. Next we embarked upon a long digression about the nature of "brains" in a beagle, and the fact that what we mean by brains can perhaps really encompass the desired traits of patience, adaptability, and independence as spelled out in the rulebook.

All the while we talked, we had lightning bugs around, and they illuminated the running grounds as the pack would come through now and again before moving over the hill and out of sight, their voices rolling through the valley and giving the illusion of a second pack chasing over by the clubhouse. Several of the beagles were wearing blinking lights on their collars to aide us in catching them when it was time to call it a night. Our philosophic discussion ended when we realized that Kenny had eaten three of those enormous burgers and the knife for slicing onions was misplaced. That problem was quickly remedied, and we began to throw the charcoal onto the campfire so as to remove any hot surface to burn the nose of a dog when we called the pack to us.

We began packing our gear and Kenny asked, "What are you going to do with that bag of ice that was in your cooler."

"Nothing, I suppose," I replied.

"Can I have it for a picnic later this summer? I will put it in my freezer at home."

"I guess so, but it might melt before you get home," I answered.

"I have an idea for that," Kenny said.

"Sounds good to me," I half didn't pay attention, as I was busy packing my things. Soon enough Kenny and Andy drove away and Renee and I got ready for camping— our plan was to run our dogs again in the morning when the skunks, coyotes, and porcupines were less active. The next day my phone rang.

"Dude." It was Andy's voice coming through the line, "The back seat of my truck is soaked. I put my shirts and stuff there, but I can't now. Did you spill soda pop or anything?"

"No, Why?"

"Man, the backseat of my truck is soaked. It's bad enough I froze the whole way home last night!" Andy growled.

"Froze? It wasn't that cold last night," I was baffled.

"Kenny kept saying he was hot and had the air conditioning jacked all the way."

"Oh," I remembered the ice. "Yeah. Kenny wanted that bag of ice. He was saving it for another picnic later in the summer."

"Whaaaat?" Andy said.

"I told him it would melt, but Kenny said he had a plan to stop that. Looks like he put it in the truck with you and turned on the AC even though it didn't cool enough to stop the melting."

Laughter erupted through the phone. Not mean-spirited laughter, but a laughter that showed a genuine appreciation for life—the sort that can happen when you are good to your neighbor and can enjoy the mishaps of real life. A compassionate laughter. We later learned that a handful of ice cubes were still surviving and placed into Kenny's freezer. On this Fourth of July, we celebrate freedom, and we remember our soldiers. We houndsmen celebrate the freedom to train our dogs and to hunt. We also celebrate the end of monarchy and a class system that was rigid and fixed as we take care of our neighbors and share the rich experiences of life with those less fortunate. We have a freedom to thrive and that freedom allows us to be generous as well.

Big Times with Small Game

In June I attended the annual gathering of the Outdoor Writers Association of America. Our keynote address on the first morning of the event was from Jonathan Jarvis, the director of the National Parks Service. The National Park system includes more than 84 million acres that you and I can use. In the keynote address, Jarvis told us that his introduction to the great outdoors occurred as a kid hunting with his father and his beagles. I also met Fred Feightner, the director of communications for Case Knives, one of the sponsors for this year's conference. I had talked to Fred on the phone before—I sent books to his father, a retired beagle who can't get in the woods as much as he once did.

Why do I mention all this? Because rabbit hunting is a big deal. Outside of our world—the world of beagling, complete with hunting and field trials—rabbit hunting is seen as a ho-hum affair. When you look at the pages of the bigger hunting and fishing magazines you see an emphasis on big game hunting, exotic locations, and expensive equipment. I would be telling you a fib if I said I do not own any shotguns that could be categorized as nice, but my first rabbit gun was a bolt action 20 gauge made by Western Auto. There may be a few youngsters reading this that never heard of a Western Auto parts store! I better explain—for the kids! Western Auto sold car parts back when a modestly coordinated person could do some maintenance on his own vehicle. This was in the olden days of the 1900s when you did not have to remove the entire air intake to reach the spark plugs, and the oil filter could be located quickly. Oh, and in addition to auto parts they sold sporting goods. It was a neatly perfect idea, but they forgot about progress.

Progress, of course, is the process of making life more complicated and causing a person to wish that things would go backwards a little bit. Ever been lost in a Wal-Mart while trying to find some small garden tool in the middle of a bunch of groceries and clothes? That's progress. It used to be that you went downtown, and there was a garden center. You didn't go there looking for groceries, unless it was in the form of future groceries, also known as seeds. There were clothing stores then too, and you could walk inside and find clothes without having to get lost in an aisle of toasters. Toasters would have been located at an appliance store. Appliance stores are really backwards because they date to a time when people fixed things. People don't do that anymore. If your iPhone doesn't work, the store tells you that you can upgrade to a new one if you promise to keep your cell phone service with them at a very expensive monthly fee. They finalize this right to a new (and fancier) phone by having you sign your soul to the store. Such evil deeds are no longer signed in blood; you simply text "Y" to the service provider and you have in effect made a nefarious deal akin to Faust's.

The same is true for having to watch a fuzzy television for a day or two until the TV repairman could come fix the thing at a fraction of the cost necessary to purchase a new boob tube. Nowadays people simply watch the show on their computer until they can go get a new, no doubt bigger, television. The only thing limiting the size of televisions is the height of the door to a house, and it would not surprise me if people started putting barn doors on the back of the house just to get a bigger screen inside. Sorry about that. I got a little carried away there.

Anytime I read the most popular hunting and fishing magazines, I feel as if I am reading a magazine devoted to people with trust funds and private jets. The advertising is for canned hunts that I cannot afford using guns as valuable as my truck. All signs seem to be pointing towards a world where hunting is the hobby of the leisure class, and none of us regular folk will get to participate—all forests will be Sherwood, and the peasants can be content elsewhere.

Not too far from where I live, there is a bird hunting preserve—the kind of place where you pay a lot of money and it entitles you to train your bird dogs and shoot a few birds with the option to pay even more money to shoot additional pen raised birds. I called and asked about a membership that just allowed me to chase rabbits without killing anything. Any cover good for birds will have rabbits too. No such membership existed, but the owner of the preserve spoke about having had beagles in his youth with pleasant fondness. It is almost as if the merry beagle is a gateway to the great outdoors before the outdoorsman moves on to bigger game in further corners of the globe.

Have you ever taken a person hunting with beagles that has never done so in the past? I once took a fellow who mostly hunts deer. We took a couple of my dogs after cottontails. He got super excited as the dog circled the rabbit past us time and time again. I could have shot the first rabbit after the second circle, but I let it pass me in the hopes that it might hop in front of my buddy. It did, and I heard a hurried volley of three shots—the maximum number of rounds permitted in a shotgun in my home state. The chase ended, and I was pretty sure he killed the rabbit. I walked over, and he was smiling—the sort of smile where you could tell he was restraining some excitement. He didn't want to look too excited at killing a rabbit at this stage in life! It wasn't shot to bits either—he had missed the first two shots entirely—a bit of rabbit fever. That can happen the first time you are waiting for the rabbit and then it suddenly appears, sneaking and streaking through the underbrush with more of its attention being given to the hounds that are baying 100 yards behind it.

Rabbit hunting is an exciting entry into becoming a sportsman. It is a way for someone to hunt with good success rates and get a lot of shooting. I realize that some people move on to fly fishing in Montana and shooting driven birds in the UK, but for many of us we remain true to our roots. Maybe there are people that look at me as if my growth ceased to develop to full potential, as if I were a guy that got so excited about the boring little rabbit that I never really moved on to enjoy more authentic hunting. I could not disagree more.

Hunting is not something to be done merely at vacation destinations—it happens relatively close to home as well. The sounds of the hounds fill the air, echo and ricochet through the hills, and provide a rhythm and melody that rivals any music on earth. When the director of the Park Service spoke of his earliest memories of beagles, he was passionate about the effect that those hounds had upon his life. Many of us that read *Better Beagling* could do the same. I do trout fish. I like to catch perch and walleye. I really enjoy deer season. Chasing spring gobblers is an activity that a friend of mine does well, and he shares his talents with me. When the weather is scorching hot, I can be found roaming the peripheries of farmers' fields in an attempt to rid their land of a few groundhogs. That brings me back to rabbits (I guess my thinking is circular, just like a rabbit's chase). Those farmers are thankful for my efforts in controlling the groundhog population, and they then allow me to come hunt bunnies. The intensity of the chase and the rolling voices of the beagles makes my soul shiver. I may chase them with a shotgun a lot more expensive than that old Western Auto bolt action, but I feel the same thrill. I have travelled as far south as Alabama to hunt swamp rabbits and as far north as the Quebec border to hunt hare, but it is no more exciting than my first cottontail hunt a short walk from my childhood home. Okay, maybe a little more exciting than my last trip hunting cottontails, but certainly not more exciting than my first hunt. I have had big time fun hunting small game.

Go to Your House!

My mother called me the instigator. I would antagonize my sister until she screamed and yelled. Then mom would punish me. "Go to your room!" she would yell at me. This was a serious punishment then, as I preferred to be outside. It was a Spartan room with a bed and a dresser and nothing else. I had no computer, no video game machine, and no stereo in that room. I did have books, and so I would kneel on the bed, put the book on the clothes dresser, and lean forward with my elbows planted on either side of the book, my hands holding my chin, and read until my jail sentence was served.

Currently I have the same sort of situation, but it is my wife who issues the punishment. You see, I can be put under house arrest. The reason this is the case is because we have two houses. When I say we have two houses, I mean that we have none. We are, however, both pastors, and the parish she serves owns a home and so does the parish I serve. I sleep in both homes, depending upon my work schedule. I am there 3-5 nights per week. There are advantages to this situation.

First is the great benefit that two houses affords me during the hunting season. If the game commission stocks pheasants in one of hunting spots, I simply stay in the house closest to that locale. When I am meeting other hunters I choose the house closest to the prearranged meeting spot. Each home has separate, but overlapping spheres of hunting spots. I keep a little dog food in each place, and I let my meeting nights, bible study schedule, and worship times dictate where the beagles and I land each night.

There are other benefits too. For instance, have you ever endured the misery of having a female beagle in heat and had to listen to the constant howling of the males? It truly is miserable. The solution to this problem occurred to us a few years ago. When I say it occurred to "us," I mean my wife and I were sleeping when the howling reached pathetic levels. The female dog of desire was locked up securely in a crate in the basement, and the male dogs began bouncing their heads off the door to the basement while howling like wolves. Renee pushed me out of bed and yelled, "Go to your house and take those evil males with you!"

So at one o'clock in the morning, I loaded the male dogs into the truck, and we drove 40 minutes to the other house. We stayed there until Princess was no longer fertile. How did I feel about the matter? Well, to be honest, I was a little dejected the first time. But consider this: what if you got to leave every six months to another location and live mostly like a bachelor? I say mostly because there are no doubt some of you that think it is some sort of time to whoop it up and chase wild women. No, you are living mostly as a bachelor. You are still married and still faithful but . . . you can eat whenever you want. Not hungry at six o'clock in the evening? No big deal, eat at eight. It is liberating to not live under regimented eating schedules. If I do not feel like cooking, no problem; I can eat breakfast cereal. Do you have any idea how angry my wife gets when she asks me what I want to eat for supper and I answer, "Cheerios" with sincere honesty?

Imagine, if you will, a bathroom that is uncluttered—no potpourri, no decorative soaps, and no towels that are off limits for drying your hands. Picture a sink top that is so free from liquid soaps, lotions, moisturizers, q-tips, nail polish, and sanitizer that you can simply set a roll of toilet paper there—I don't even use the toilet paper holder! This is my bathroom. It is like being in college again, only without the aggravation of roommates. It is just me and the hunting beagles.

Having two bases of operation is also a joy for field trials. They are 40 minutes apart, and I stay wherever I can sleep in a little extra. Additionally I can drive home and just relax after a long Saturday chasing beagles at a trial. Beagle clubs may or may not be located near big highways, so I see which house is closer in terms of time to the field trial destination, rather than distance. It works great.

The greatest advantage, however, is now over. That was the mail. I sometimes get an urge to shop online, mostly beagle stuff. I get beagle decals, leashes, and things like that. Sometimes I see a really nice pair of hunting boots on sale and I click a few buttons and, with the beauty of two-day free shipping, I am walking in the high weeds with dry feet. I have a few "hick" things as my wife calls them—a bolo tie made with a photo of my beagles chasing a rabbit, a belt with beagles on it, a pocket watch with hounds chasing a rabbit, a case knife with beagles etched into the handle, and a billfold with—you guessed it—beagles on it! I simply had the packages delivered to MY HOUSE!

My woes began in large part because my house (actually the church owns it) is in a town so small that no one gets mail delivered to their home. Everyone has a P.O. Box. That made life difficult enough as they were only open from 8:30-4:15. Two-day shipping, however, meant I could predict the day the package would arrive. I mean, Amazon tells me when it is going to arrive! So I would rush about and do my work and manage to get to the post office by 4:10 in the afternoon. Perfect. Then rural post offices all around me began shutting down. Eventually the one in my town went to half day service, but with all day access to the P.O Box. The only problem was that you can't get a package after noon. You need to be there when a human being is there to pick up a package, and that means before noon. So I began having my little goodies shipped to my other house, the one my wife stays in all the time.

It turns out that I get one of these little goodies every ten days, on average. The average cost is somewhere in the neighborhood of $20. This amounts to $730 dollars per year. I can prove this to you because she created a spreadsheet with itemized lines and estimated expenses due to inflation. She was intercepting my mail, or as she called it, getting home first because I was too busy running dogs!

She felt that this sort of an expense for tacky dog stuff was not needed, especially when $730 could be utilized in going out to dinner and giving her a break from cooking supper. I offered to cook supper, but she felt that Cheerios was not a good choice. I even explained that I could get fancy and make Shredded Wheat, but she still refused. I am left with only one choice: I have to purchase big ticket items like boots whenever Princess is in heat, and I will definitely be at the other house for a solid week. She is due any week now, and I need a new pair of snowshoes. . . .

Buckets of Vork

Not long ago my wife, Renee, said, "Do you want to go run dogs at the beagle club together tonight?" When we first got married, I would have been elated at hearing this request. I might have hugged her and jumped up and down in real excitement. "Well?" she held her arms out to the side, palms facing up, as if to question why I had not yet gone into full excitement mode. She knows I love to run dogs, and she also doesn't often ask to go with me.

"Maybe," I pulled on my beard and scratched my head. While desperately trying to determine what she wanted. I belong to two clubs—which one did she mean? I frantically thought through all of the stores on the way to Bellwood— was there anything that was appealing to her shopping sensibilities? Lion Country Supply was the only store I could recall, other than gas stations. She doesn't shop there. I did the same for West Branch. Did she want to go to the Woolrich Store? That's an all day venture if she did. I must have been mulling over these potential time traps for quite some time.

"DO YOU WANT TO GO?" she yelled.

"Sure," I answered more as a question than an affirmation. "I will get the hounds loaded."

Getting hounds loaded is a multistage process at my house. The first stage is tricking my old retired Rebel into a crate in the basement. This is because he always got to go with me, no matter what, for twelve years. I rotated what other hounds went, but Old Rebel is a check dog! He rarely lost a rabbit. He made the starting lineup every single time I went. He has been retired, or mostly retired, because he just can't go with my younger dogs. His body has many miles of thorns and swamps under his paws. He howls when he sees me loading dogs, and it is pathetically depressing. So I have to make sure that he doesn't see me carrying his younger kennel mates (some are his progeny) to the truck's dog box.

Next, I put collars on the dogs I am taking. Sometimes I put my old SportDOG Tek 1.0 tracking collars (without the training modules) on them. Other times, I use the new Tek 2.0 tracking & training collars. Much of the time I actually take the handheld remotes too! I often will let them run without even activating the collars. All my dogs know is that the E collars are a sign that we are going to run rabbits. They have no idea what they do. On the rare occasion that I have to correct a dog, they don't realize that the stimulation is from the collar; it is from me. I mostly use the tracking function, in case they run out of hearing. They associate the collar with the joy of getting to go into the truck, that magical box that transports them to the rabbits! They love those collars. I am sure we have all seen dogs that see the training collars as a punishment. That is not my goal.

Anyway, the hunting house hounds get collared on the back of the easy chair. I retrieved the tracking collars from my office and brought them into the living room. Hoss, Duke, and Badger did the happy dance, twirling in place when they saw them. Then they jumped onto the chair, more specifically, they balanced on the back of it. From there, they stand chest high to me, jostling one another to make sure they are going to get a collar and go—even though they almost always go as a trio and no one gets left behind. I finished loading the dogs and I noticed that a couple buckets were in the bed of my truck.

That took some keen observation skills too, as anyone who has ever seen my truck bed can tell you that it is full of tie out stakes, chains, miscellaneous empty soda pop bottles, folding lawn chairs, and a couple chunks of apple wood that I will eventually bring into the garage in order to make wood chips for smoking venison sausage. But, no, I clearly noticed two buckets and I could not for the life of me remember when I put those in there.

"It's blackberry season," my wife said as she jumped into the passenger seat of my truck. A wave of psychological trauma washed over my body as childhood memories became as vivid and real as if they happened yesterday. Kids today have to be tricked into doing work. Rewards are offered, and various tactics are used to make the work sound like fun. "Hey Buddy," a parent says (all kids are called Buddy), "wouldn't it be fun for me to use a watch and time how long it takes you to pick up your toys and put them in your toy box?"

The kid looks at dad and smiles, "Okay!"

"Sounds good, Buddy! On your mark, get set, go!" Dad leaps with fake excitement. Buddy walks to one of the toys, picks it up, and starts playing with it. "Faster, Buddy! You are in a race!" Dad yells and puts a few toys in the box. Buddy ignores Dad, despite the constant, loud, but pleasant encouragements that never come close to sounding like a warning of impending punishment. Twenty minutes later, Dad has put all the toys away except the one that Buddy is using.

Parents never did this in the past. My dad would say, "If I step on one of those toys, you are going to be sorry," and walk away. I would have them all picked up in about 32 seconds. I knew what Dad meant by "Sorry." My grandmother, however, was the source of psychological trauma that washed over me when I spied the buckets in my truck. Gram would send my sister and me out to pick berries when she stopped to visit us. Sometimes, however, we would be sent to her house as indentured servants. Mom would drop us off, and Gram would come give hugs and tell Mom when to come get us. Then, we would wave at Mom as she drove out of sight, before we heard, "Alright! Get Zees buckets, it is time to vork!" It was like a WWII German stalag, and we were in trouble. We would drive to various orchards and farms where you could pick your own berries at a reduced price.

"Only pick zee ripest berries! VORK!" Sis and I would scramble to pick as fast as we could. We were at one farm that had immigrants picking the berries that would be sold in the farmer's store. "Slow down, kid," one of the migrant pickers said to me. "You are making me look bad!"

"Sorry," I said, "my gram is watching." Pharaoh had no task master as brutal as Gram. Had Moses risen up in righteous indignation against her, she would have yelled, "Don't you look at me that way!" and then quoted some obscure bible verse about the need to work. Every day we filled a five- gallon bucket. Then Gram would take us into town for ice cream and pretend that she was sweet. "These kids are so cute, and they are here for a week this summer. They do so well in school and never have to be yelled at to do homework." Her Zees became these, and vork became work in public. Her eyes even became brown instead of fiery red. Every morning it was berries, and every afternoon it was theater for the masses.

Blackberry season was always the worst. She would send us crawling into the briars to retrieve the big "shade berries" that were so far into the thickets that only the bears could reach them, the briars unable to penetrate their thick hides. "Just crawl through zat opening and pick zee big berries!" she would motion me into the thorns the way I do my beagles. Naturally I couldn't drag a bucket in there, so I would hold my shirt by the bottom hem and fill it until my belly was exposed as the shirt cradled a quart of bursting fruit. Then it was time to slowly back out of the briars, real low to the ground, hoping that a thorn didn't tear into my back, just to dump them into the five-gallon bucket that she planted just outside the berry patch. I would crawl back in, like a coal miner without enough room to stand.

Gram was picking her share too, even more in fact. She had grandmother fingers—bent and twisted from all the sewing, quilting, crocheting, and whatever other sorts of repetitive actions had made her knuckles and fingers gnarled. All grandmothers had hands like that. She could fill a bucket in half the time as us kids.

"Are you ready?" my wife got out of the truck and saw me staring at the buckets.

"Yeah," I said. West Branch is the only club I belong to that has blackberries. They have thick briars too. And they are on a hill. My wife probably wouldn't make me pick berries like Gram did, but I would help anyway. It is amazing how much faster the work goes with the sound of hounds chasing a rabbit.

"Good, I don't want to be gone all night," she said. "I have to vork in the morning."

STARING INTO SPACE

"What are you doing?" my wife, Renee, said to me.

"Writing," I answered.

"To me it looks like you are staring into space," Renee countered.

"That's a big part of writing," I explained.

"You must be writing all the time," she smiled. One of those smiles that are kind of mean, you know the one? More of a sneer.

"No, sometimes I am daydreaming. That is almost like writing."

"You mean when you get all nostalgic and wish that the TV only had 4 channels and that Pepsi still came in glass bottles?"

"Exactly," as I stared off into space—I mean wrote.

I do get nostalgic for old times. And I am not that old. The most common thing I hear when I meet people at field trials is, "I thought you'd be older."

My friend, Joe, has always told me that I am old and crotchety before my time. But I miss the old times. Especially with dogs. I miss those old dogs that have passed away and provided me with such great memories. I can sit and remember a chase with perfect recall. Well, maybe better than perfect recall. A memory is so much more than a video. When kids perform in plays at school or pageants for church, I always feel bad for the parent that is video recording the entire event, being a spectator though a lens. I sometimes wonder how often they ever watch that video again. Besides, the school or church usually makes a recording of the big event, and you can get a copy pretty easy. It seems that they miss it all, for the sake of preserving it on digital bytes.

It is a fact that beagling has gone into social media. And I am one of the biggest culprits. I post pictures and videos on Facebook quite often. Beagles are my one true passionate hobby. I don't have cable, don't care to go to restaurants, and have gaping holes in my knowledge of pop culture. I had no idea who the Kardashians were until their step dad decided to become a woman and one of my church members called me to ask me about it.

"Wait, wait wait," I said. "You lost me. We are talking about the guy that was on the cover of the Wheaties cereal box, right?"

"He's not a guy anymore. Well she is, except she now has breast implants and wears women's clothes, and shaved the Adam's apple."

"Oh," I said and could not have cared less. I went to a minor league baseball game and did not know any of the songs that they played in between batters and after foul balls. Beagles are my one hobby and maybe a little hunting of other wild game and a bit of fishing. So, yeah, I will use social media to promote my hounds and books. I worry, though, that documenting hounds can get in the way of enjoying them. Like the poor dad who missed his kid's performance in the pageant because he was so glued to the video recorder. A little sad, really. I totally understand the value in these endeavors, and there are hounds I owned in my youth that I would love to have on video chasing rabbits just to hear their voice one more time and experience the thrill of their hunts.

Dead hounds get better with time. I remember their great talents and get amnesic about their faults. I have memories of their pursuits of Peter Cottontail that are better than a video. There are memories that include smells, the feel of a cold wind, or the moisture of a sweaty face in the sun.

I use GPS collars all the time now, and I went to run dogs not too long ago and realized that I forgot to bring the tracking collars. I ALMOST turned around to go home. Then I thought, "What would my dad say if he was alive and I told him that I went home because I forgot a collar connected to a satellite?"

I thought about my first beagle, Duke, and all the great chases that we had and how much fun I had with him and a half littermate that my dad bought at the same time— with no GPS. I vividly remembered how my father made my buy my first dog with my money, so as to prove that I was committed to taking care of the hound and was able to demonstrate the responsibility necessary to train and own a hunting dog.

My first rabbit kill came flooding back to me with such intensity that I remembered the smell of the apples rotting on the ground that day, and the smell of the damp oak leaves where I field dressed that first bunny. Such wonderful memories, and then I thought of other dogs that have died.

I thought of Bandit, a dog that went from fit as a fiddle to dead from cancer in very, very short order. He was incontinent at the end, and I slept on the linoleum floor of the kitchen with him, praying that he would pass in the night before I had to take him to my veterinarian, who told me he had a massive tumor, the kind that grows very quickly, and there was nothing I could have done or noticed. I held him as he was euthanized. I was overcome with emotion thinking about my Lady Day, or "Guts and Go" as I called her because of her desire and ability to will rabbits out of brush piles on any day, even when no other dog could jump a bunny. I love the way she would hop on her back legs in tall goldenrod, using her eyes to look for a bunny that she smelled on the wind at a distance. I remember taking her collar off her lifeless body when she was euthanized due to cancer too, and how soaked my shirt was with tears from holding her for her last breaths.

I forced myself to remember all these dogs in healthier times, and their great enthusiasm for the chase, and I could hear their voices rolling off the hills and echoing though the valleys. Joy and thanksgiving replaced sorrow.

"Hello!!!!" My wife was yelling at me.

"What?" I said.

"Supper is ready," she explained. "Didn't you hear me?"

"I guess not. Sorry."

"That's okay. Were you daydreaming or writing or staring into space?" she asked. I thought fondly of all my dogs and remembered some of their best chases. "Well, which was it?" she asked again.

"They are all the same," I smiled and got misty eyed all at once as hound music filled my soul.

You Will Grow into Them

It is that time of year when kids are returning to school. I always dreaded the first day of school, and I despised shopping for school clothes. It was an annual ritual where my mom would drag me and my sister to the shopping mall, and we were outfitted for the fall. My sister liked this day, and I was decidedly indifferent. I had my clothes in an hour. As long as it fit, I wore it. The first day of school had kids with brand new blue jeans and squeaky new sneakers on the linoleum hallways.

"You'll grow into it," Mom would say when I was in elementary school. She tried to buy my pants a little long and my shirts a little baggy so that they would last until Santa brought new duds at Christmas. Mom would feel for my toe in my new school shoes to make sure that they were almost, but not quite, too big. "You'll grow into them," she would say. The same was true for my first hunting vest. It looked almost like a blaze orange dress due to the fact that it hung so low.

"Gee, Dad," I said, "the pockets are so low that I have trouble getting shotgun shells out of them."

"You will grow into it," he patted me on the back.

My first pair of hunting boots came with three pairs of wool socks—not from the same store, mind you. "These boots feel big," I said.

"Nope, they are just right," Dad said. "You need to wear three pairs of socks to stay warm, and they will fit perfectly then." I, of course, believed him.

When the next deer season came around, I was worried because my boots were too tight. "Well, you have three pairs of wool socks on your feet!" Dad yelled. "Take two pairs off."

"But Dad," I said, "I won't be able to keep my feet warm."

"What in the heck are you walking about?" my father sighed impatiently.

"You said I need three pairs of socks to keep my feet warm," I held my hand out with three fingers extended to visually emphasize my point.

"That's crazy. When did I say that?"

"Last year when I got these boots."

"Oh, well you are older now, so you will be able to stay warm just fine with one pair of socks."

My friends from larger families had it even worse. They wore hand-me-downs, and sometimes the age difference between brothers was a little bit too far for a good fit. My one buddy always had suspenders on his hunting pants because no belt in the world could tighten the waist line enough. He had cuffs in his pants that went halfway to his knees.

"Those are way too big!" I said.

"Yeah," he sighed, "and I am wearing three pairs of long johns . . ."

The church next to our house has a ministry called the Mommy Shop. You can trade in the clothes that your baby just outgrew for the next size. They have clothes ranging from newborn to toddler. It is a very popular ministry, and I can see why.

When my wife and I got married, I acquired a stepson. He was still in elementary school, and I will never forget the first time we went shopping for clothes. "Why do his blue jeans cost more than mine?" I asked my wife.

"Because you wear Wrangler jeans," my wife, Renee, rolled her eyes.

"What's wrong with Wrangler?"

"Nothing," she sighed, "but they are less expensive for sure."

"There ain't enough denim on his whole pair of pants to make one leg on mine. They should be cheaper."

"Prices on clothes have nothing to do with sizes," she explained to me in a condescending way that you might utilize to point out the obvious to someone.

"That's not true," I pointed at her. "XXL shirts always cost a few dollars more!"

"Well," she put her hands on her hips, "of course they do. They are bigger, and use more fabric."

"Right," I said, "I am saying the same thing about the little kid jeans."

"No, it doesn't work that way," she pointed out an obvious fact. Which seemed more like a contradiction to me.

"Well, buy them a little long and a bit big in the waist and get some suspenders."

"I can't send him to school in suspenders!" she yelled. "He needs clothes that fit."

"He will grow into them," I said, and suddenly my mom and dad made sense to me.

"I will not have him being teased!"

"Why?" I asked. "Teasing is a big part of childhood. It is 90% of their social interactions."

"That can't be true," Renee rolled her eyes again. "What is the other 10% of their social time?"

"Fighting and playing sports."

"You are old fashioned. Kids wear clothes that fit. And they get in trouble for teasing each other in school. They can be suspended for it."

"No wonder they keep laying off teachers from schools. There must not be that many kids in class with all of the teasing violations."

"We are going to get his sneakers at a different store," she changed the topic.

"Okay, but I saw socks were on sale here. I will buy a bunch and we can get his shoes a half size too big." She just walked away.

Recently I saw some puppies and was excited about the idea of maybe getting a new one myself. Then I was talking pedigrees with a buddy, and we are thinking we might just breed one of my males with one of his females—the pedigrees and running style matched up well for us. There is something about big floppy ears and clumsy feet on a pup that just melts my heart and fills me with hope. Whenever a pup trips over its own feet I always have the same thought: "He will grow into them."

How Long Have We Been Here?

On one of those rare summer evenings where the temperatures are cool and the humidity was low, Lenny and I were running our dogs at the beagle club. We had a very cooperative rabbit that was leading the dogs on gigantic, squared-off circles with very few turns and even fewer checks. The sun was low in the sky, and we decided to walk back to the tailgate and have a little chit chat about some upcoming hunting plans.

We talked about places we might travel, guns we might take, and possible combinations of our dogs to form a pack to hunt all day! The next thing I knew, it was dark. It was the kind of dark that sends you scrambling into the truck to find a flashlight so that you can catch the dogs. "How long have we been here?" I asked Lenny. A question that reminded us both of another time we were conditioning dogs in the evening.

A couple years ago, Lenny and I ventured into the brush with nothing but a cell phone for light, and said phone had a battery that was rapidly depleting. It was fully depleted by the time we caught the dogs and took them off the rabbit they were chasing. We decided to find our way back to the truck by waiting for the clouds to occasionally part and show us the moon, which Lenny knew would take us to the road where we were parked.

When that failed, we walked until we hit the fence line of the beagle club. I knew if we followed the fence line it would led us to the gate, even if it was a longer route. It was better than stumbling around the club. Hey, I have seen plenty of dogs that do the same thing inside beagle club enclosures. I am not sure how those dogs are utilized in hunting season.

I now keep a couple flashlights in the truck, so that I can always find at least one of them. So, having learned my lesson a couple years ago, I retrieved a flashlight from the truck, utterly shocked at how late it was. Perhaps you too have noticed how quickly time passes when you are having fun. I have had the same experience while fishing. The trout are rising, the action is fast, and the catches are plentiful. The next thing I know I am following a stream in the pitch black night air with the limbs of the trees that overhang the river knocking my hat off my head and the rod out of my hand.

This is the nature of fun. I remember how quickly gym class seemed to fly by and how French class felt like a prison sentence. I find the same to be true when I go shopping with my wife. Granted, I do not do this very often. I go at Christmas, when she spends a marathon day in the mall looking for thoughtful and useful gifts for people that we know. There is a bench there, near a fountain, where I sit and wait for her to bring a bag of goodies which I then shuttle to the car as she bounds away towards the next purchasing conquest. I return to the fountain after I come back inside from my shuttle run to the car. I could follow her, but there is no point. She slips in and out of rows of merchandise, and I can't get through those same openings. Moreover, she has an uncanny ability to move amongst other shoppers and dart between them as they converge, not at all unlike a skilled running back in football that just knows what the tacklers are going to do next. For my part, I feel like a linebacker, caught behind the play, who is unable to follow her due to the randomly moving shoppers, their carts, and the rows and shelves of goods for sale. Before I know it she is gone, into the briars of the commercial world and I cannot relocate her. If I am lucky she will re-emerge as suddenly as she entered the shadows of shopping, but this is unlikely. Sitting on that bench by the fountain is the best choice I have, though I tend to eat too much mall food as I wait. I like the pretzels. Also the cookies. And the Orange Julius. Well, the candy isn't too bad either, if I am honest. The one stand has good coffee too. Don't judge me; what would you do with all that time waiting in between trips to the parking lot?

Speaking of my wife, the first year after we were married it was June, and I knew her birthday was coming soon. I just didn't know what day. So I sent her kid, my stepson, to fetch the driver's license from her purse so I would know what day to get her a gift. I would shop alone, of course, which would mean it could be done quickly. My thought was that it would be better for the kid to get caught rummaging through the purse than me. The problem with this plan, of course, is that purses are one of the great mysteries of the universe insofar as the interior volume is approximately quadruple the amount of space as you would expect if you measured the external dimensions.

My stepson had to unpack the entire contents of the purse to find the driver's license. He had trouble reloading it. By the time I crammed all the contents back into the thing (who carries that many pens?) it no longer had the sleek look it once did. It looked pregnant. Or maybe just constipated. In any case, it looked capable of purging some volume at any moment, and I feared that my wife would be suspicious. She was.

"Were you in my purse?" my wife asked later that day.

I momentarily considered being truthful—and tell her that the kid had done it. But that would merely invite more questions, which would invite more truth. "Yes," I answered.

"Did you need some money?" she asked.

"What?"

"You always ask me for quarters when you are going to be parking downtown because they are the only coins that the meters take." She unwittingly suggested my alibi.

"Yes," I said, feeling it much better to be known as the guy that stole quarters from his wife than the guy that did not know his wife's birthday.

"Well, there are always quarters in the plastic cup on top of the refrigerator too," she cheerfully attended to my parking needs. She opened the purse, made what appeared to be a magician's wave of the hand, and the purse looked as if it had had a large belch, and all of the contents slid into place and looked much more comfortable.

We are into September as you read this, and I know for a fact this is our wedding anniversary month. I even know the date, as I do her birthday as well now. I wasn't sure how many years we had been married until a few weeks ago. I had to do some research on that. I was embarrassed that I did not know—I was within a couple years, but my initial guess was wrong. I had to look in our wedding album to figure it out—much easier than unpacking a purse and way less complicated than repacking the same purse.

Now that I think about it, it makes sense that I wasn't sure how long we have been married. We have been married longer than I thought, so it goes to the maxim that time flies when you are having fun. As a beagler, I can say that she has been fantastic. She has whelped three litters for me. She was at the vet's office for an emergency C-Section breathing life into pups, helping the vet as she did the same. When life isn't too busy she will run dogs with me, though she isn't fond of early morning chases—more a fan of evening runs.

We hunt hare near her hometown in upstate New York, and her main duty is to stay between the dogs and the highway to ensure that no dogs get onto the road. She does the same thing on some hunting trips here at home in Pennsylvania.

"You seem a little stressed," she said to me one time when my duties as a parish pastor were particularly depressing with a rash of illnesses and funerals. "Why don't you go run the dogs and I will take care of things here at home?" She has done this on several occasions since then.

Last spring she handled dogs at a field trial. The pack was picked up with 5 dogs still running the rabbit, meaning my dog placed. "I don't know how your dog did," Harry Breon said, "but your wife was in the brush handling your dog better than anyone out there!"

Then there is the mud from boots, the dog hair, tangled knot of leashes, the stacks of beagle magazines, and all the other things that are typical for a beagler. It may even be more difficult for her than most wives, as my pack lives in the house! She loves being with the hounds and will groom their coats and check their ears. I hate to give the impression that she does everything with the dogs, but it seems that way sometimes. She lets me know when we need dog food, and she will feed them at night when I have meetings. She even remembers their birthdays! She told me last fall, "Today is Shadow's birthday. We are having mashed potatoes for supper. I know that you do not like mashed potatoes, but Shadow loves them." Every dog gets a special treat on their birthday.

And so, it is with great fondness that I am overcome with joy to be married to Renee, and I ask myself "How long have we been here?" Good times have that effect on us.

LIFE LESSONS

It occurs to me that there are some life lessons that beagles have taught me over the years. It is no secret that the best way to learn about rabbit dogs is to own a good one. Old Rover (or Sport, or Spot, or whatever the name) is a much better tutor about rabbit hunting than any book or video. This goes doubly true for Youtube videos, which seems to be full of footage that is prepared by guys that want to help anti-hunters as they film unethical shots and moronic commentary that belittles the beautiful creation of God that we hunt. No, observing beagles is the best way to learn about the sport. I also feel, however, that our dogs are able to teach us about much more than hunting.

I started talking to my wife, Renee, the other day, as I have done countless times, and she erupted in rage. Now, I should point out that I was talking in a weird voice, very loudly while clapping my hands and teasing her. After she yelled, I promptly ignored her since she had no reason to act so rudely. I found out later that she was on her cell phone in the middle of a very important call. I didn't see the small phone so I was unaware that I had actually been the rude one in this encounter. It took all day until I figured this out!

By contrast, one of my dogs, Duke, crawled up next to my on the couch in pursuit of a little attention and scratched my chest with his toenails. The nails were not long, but I was lying on my back watching a ballgame on the television, and he managed to stab me where my chest turns into belly. I yelled and screamed and off he ran. A few minutes later, he walked back. The poor dog wasn't sure what he had done, as he has crawled up on my chest a gabillion times to get a scratch behind the ear. He approached with tail tucked, and I welcomed him into my arms where he flopped on my stomach and quickly moved to nap mode as I twirled his long ears. That dog was so eager to make amends, regardless of who was at fault! Too often, it seems, people wait too long to seek reconciliation when my dogs know that harmony is important.

There are few things as restful as a beagle after a long rabbit chase. They focus on their passion for rabbits and work hard. When they come home, they sleep without a worry in the world. I come home from work and continue to worry about it. What if a church member went to the hospital and I did not know? They tend to get mad if the pastor doesn't visit, and sometimes everyone thinks that someone else told me about the illness when in fact no one did. What should I do about a dispute between a few parishioners over the best way to spend the memorial fund money? Given the recent cable news (all bad), how should I preach the good news?

Not my hounds. They do their best each day and sleep without a solitary concern. Surely, they do work hard too. They are tireless in the brush, entering every thicket that looks likely to hold game, and pursuing rabbits with desire and determination. I've owned a few beagles that are beyond difficult to catch when it is time to go home. They will run until exhaustion if I allow them. They love to go to work! Every once in a while I wake up with dread about a day of work. Maybe a church member is getting ready to enter eternity, and I am overcome with grief that temporarily blinds me to resurrection. Some days are filled with great challenge—natural disasters, drug overdose, house fires, automobile accidents, homicide, and suicide have all been terrible events that I have had to walk into and offer compassion. Beagles have taught me that these things can be endured for the good times. There are baptisms, weddings, anniversaries, graduations, picnics, bible studies, and worship. Beagles never seem to mind the greenbrier, crusty snow, multi-floral rose, or any other obstacle that must be endured to chase rabbits. They gladly work hard in difficult circumstances.

By nature, we are competitive. We want to be the best, or at least better than someone! I sometimes wonder if this is why people seem to be happy about scandal—it's great to see someone that had it so good now feeling so bad. I know many people that read the newspaper (for you youngsters, that is how people got the news before cable television) by starting with the obituaries and the police report! The entire process of getting hired for a job is about looking better than the next person. I was at a job interview once and was asked, "Why are you the best person for this job?"

"I'm not sure that I am," I said, not really caring if I got the job. "I don't know who else you interviewed." The hiring committee got a chuckle out of that remark. They gave me the job. A pack of beagles loves chasing the rabbit, and while some may compete hard for the front, they all work as a team and no beagle walks away just because they aren't the best one there. They all contribute as they can. Maybe one dog is a specialist at finding a rabbit. Some have better noses. Others have more patience for the difficult tricks. Beagles chasing rabbits are the best display of cooperation that I have experienced.

Sometimes we go astray. Years ago, before GPS and Mapquest, I got lost looking for a meeting in another town. Not the kind of lost where I might starve, but the kind of lost where I was in the general region of the destination but was circling an area that comprised a few blocks looking for the exact address. I saw a used book store. I enjoy bookstores, so I thought I would go inside and take a quick look around before asking an employee for directions. My goodness was the store large! The books were separated by category, but those various classifications were packed into shelves and book cases that sprawled around corners and oozed across rooms. Then I smelled coffee! When I was a kid they had the four food groups; then they changed that to the food pyramid. I say the bottom layer of the pyramid is coffee.

Sure enough, a hot cup of Joe on a cold day was the right remedy to look through all those books. I found an old Gene Hill book, a biblical commentary, a decent collection of poems, a Karl Barth text, a Greek New Testament, and few philosophy books that all became essential contributions to my library. It took two cups of coffee to browse the entire store. Oh, I showed up at the meeting just as it ended. And Methodists don't have short meetings, so I must have been in that bookstore for a couple hours. The good news is that I missed a meeting; the bad news is that I got off the trail.

The truth is that I can get off track pretty easy. Just when I think I am eating healthy, some kindly parishioner offers me a slab of pie with ice cream when I visit, and I don't have the willpower to say no. If I forget to clean the clutter from my desk one day, it can last for weeks until I have more books on the desk than on the shelves. I can be on my way to do something important, and someone will stop me to talk and I get absorbed in the conversation, only to forget what I was going to do next. A beagle always looks for trail when it is lost. I love watching a pack of hounds work a check and keeping the rabbit on the run. The second they lose contact with the scent trail the only thing that matters is finding it again. So often we have serious side tracks in life where we get off the trail and onto depression, grief, anger, greed, and other distractions can pull us away from the trail of faith. Beagles remind me to always keep after the important thing in life. This is why I created a list of life lessons learned from beagles.

1. Go to the woods every day.
2. Be passionate about what you do.
3. Do your best while honoring the pack.
4. Be happy. Make up after a disagreement.
5. Work hard. Beating the brush gets results.
6. Sleep is important. Fluff the blanket. Spin in circles.
7. Snacks. Run another rabbit to make room for snacks.
8. When you lose the trail, passionately search until it is found.
9. If you are excited, show it.
10. Chase after what matters in life and sing to the world.

I know that beagles can also be gluttonous, loud, stubborn, and smelly. Perhaps I will write another list that focuses on these things, but for today I am happy to point to the life lessons that the merry beagle has shared with me.

Autumn Dinner Party

The thing about autumn is that I look forward to it the same way school kids look forward to summer. I would go so far as to say that I look forward to autumn with the same excitement that kids have for Christmas. Heck, I would go even further and say that I look forward to autumn with the same maniacal zeal that retailers have when they look forward to Christmas. I am not exaggerating in the slightest by telling you that the arrival of fall is met with the same sense of relief for me as housemothers once had on the first day of school.

My mom was a housemother. House moms aren't as common now, but they basically worked 24 hours per day. My mom could iron clothes and smack me on the bottom at the same time. I always worried that she would smack me with the clothes iron by mistake, but she always used the free hand or her foot, often without looking up from the garment that was losing its wrinkles. "Stop instigating!" she would boot my behind as I walked past. She often called me The Instigator, as I would tease my sister.

Mom loved the first day of school. I think that, in those days, housemothers all gathered for a victory breakfast at some restaurant on the first day of school as soon as we kids were ushered out the door to get the bus. When I say ushered, I mean pushed out the door so that we could walk to the bus stop that was a couple streets away. We didn't get a ride in the family car or an escort from our mothers. We entered the mayhem of society. We had to navigate our way past mean dogs that people tied out in their lawns with enough chain to reach the street's sidewalk. It seemed like everybody had a dog tied in the yard to keep kids from taking shortcuts.

The morning commute to the bus stop had other hazards. There were roads to cross. "Make sure you look both ways when you cross that main street," Dad warned us, "because if you get hit by a car, I will beat your butt!" Only he didn't say butt. I was always careful to look both ways before crossing the street. The last thing I wanted was to get hit by a car and be hospitalized. It would be embarrassing to get spanked in front of all those nurses and doctors. Kids aren't allowed to cross roads anymore, but they probably would not be afraid to do it. There isn't much embarrassment in being given a timeout in front of the nurses. A kid would no sooner be allowed to cross a road today than walk the entire Appalachian Trail on a solo trek. They would be too busy playing a handheld video game to look for traffic.

By far, however, the biggest hazard was other kids. No adults walked their kids to the bus stop. Every day was a renewed endeavor of strife as kids worked out a pecking order that created a hierarchy of social status. Verbal insults, pushing, shoving, hair pulling, punching, and even swinging book bags as weapons were common. Well, maybe not common, but not unexpected. I once saw a kid get smacked by a garbage can lid that was being wielded like a shield. I shrugged my shoulders in silent appreciation. This strife happened every single day. It was like the movie *Groundhog Day*. If *Groundhog Day* was more like *Lord of the Flies*. Anyway, I am pretty sure that our mothers ran to a restaurant and had breakfast, thankful to pay someone to cook for them and to sit and eat a meal in peace, and even have someone bring them coffee or tea.

That is how I anticipate autumn. What a glorious time of the year. The scenting conditions improve and the rabbits are full grown, and there are grouse, woodcock, and pheasant to shoot as well. It is just perfect. Now, I will admit, that it puts a damper on supper with my wife. I hunt until dark and then get the dogs fed and watered before changing clothes. Even when I try not to be late, it happens. The dogs will be on a screaming hot chase, and I wait for the shot—what better way to catch the dogs than shooting the rabbit?

The church I serve has even become accustomed to me rushing into a 7 pm meeting wearing bibs and boots and the beagles snooze in the dog box. All throughout the hot, miserable summer I check the weather forecast, rejoicing in cold fronts and all day rains when I can take the dogs out and let them chase. When fall arrives and the gift of frost nips the grass, I get excited. The dogs can roll! The frost also brings relief from my seasonal allergies that start in late summer and last until the first hard freeze. Until then I walk around in an antihistamine-induced haze in a futile attempt to thwart the sneezing and stuffiness. Sometimes I take allergy medicine for the sneezing and then extra coffee to counteract the sleepiness that the medicine induces.

Frosty grass and dried leaves are my best friends. No more allergy meds. Melting frost is as good as dew for tracking scent, and listening to beagles ramble over hills and through valleys makes me feel more alive than anything. As I mentioned, I tend to be tardy for evening engagements this time of year. Last year my wife said that I had to go to a dinner party.

"I don't want to go," I said. "It is hunting season."

"No problem," she moved her arms in the same way that a football referee might indicate that a team is refusing a penalty. "You can just come to dinner from the woods, whenever you are done."

"This is a trick," I bit my lip trying to figure out the trap.

"Nope," she said. "It is very informal, just graze and walk. There is no time to arrive or leave. I will meet you there. You come when you can."

"I will have to take care of the dogs and change clothes first."

"Can't you take dog food with you?" she asked.

"Why?"

"The dinner is at Mary's house," she said, "So why don't you drive there, and then feed the dogs in their truck box the way you sometimes do and just come inside?"

"I will have boots and bibs on," I said. "They aren't going to want me in the house like that."

"Its fine," she waved her hand at me like shooing a fly. "There are other guys coming from the woods that night too. Like I said, it's very informal."

"Oh, yeah?" I perked up. "I didn't know any of your friends had husbands that hunted."

"Some," she said.

I almost forgot about the dinner party, to be honest, but my wife sent 471 text messages throughout the day to remind me. Some of the texts told me to put dog food in the truck. Others reminded me that I could come anytime. One suggested I wear clean socks. One said to bring ice to keep the rabbits chilled until we got home from the meal. There were many more, but I can't remember them all.

The hunting was great, and I could tell right away that I was going to test the limits of "Come whenever you are done hunting."

I shot three rabbits, the last one at dusk. Then I had the long drive to Mary's house. I couldn't quite remember which house was Mary's, because she and her husband live on a cul-de-sac where every house looks identical. I had nothing to fear, however, as the house had cars parked all over the yard. I walked in, and much to my dismay it was a Halloween party.

Halloween parties, in my mind, are for kids. When adults have Halloween parties, the men dress weird and the women dress as various sorts of prostitutes. This seems like an odd thing, especially since we are middle aged. Some guys get a sports car for a mid-life crisis. Others buy a shotgun. I bought a tracking collar. It seems that many women like to work out at the gym and then wear skimpy clothes in public.

"Dude, what is that awesome costume?" a guy I never met asked me.

"It's not a cost—" I started.

"Are you a lumberjack?"

"No," I answered. So there I stood in knee high leather boots, brush pants, a chamois shirt, and a ball cap as the guy bombarded me with guesses as to my costume.

"Hi, honey," my wife appeared, dressed as a librarian prostitute. I think.

"A Halloween party?" I asked. "Who organized this?"

"Some of the trophy wives. They stay home with the kids all day, and they get bored."

"Wait," I said, "you mean housemothers organized this hedonism?"

"No," she shooed away my words. "Housewives do housework. These are gals that have maids and gardeners."

"We know people that have maids?"

"It's a fundraiser to help a family. I knew you wouldn't come if I told you." She looked over her glasses. "The food is all outside on the patio."

I mingled for a bit. I ate some tiny hamburgers and some cheese cubes that were cut smaller than necessary. I saw no other hunters, until one guy approached me in full camo. He looked as bewildered as I did. "Hey," he said to me. "Were you hunting? My wife said there were going to be hunters here."

"My wife said that too," I answered.

"Which prostitute is your wife?" he asked, and then looked scared. "I don't mean to say your wife is a-a-a-a-a-a-a, so sorry . . ."

"Relax," I patted him on the back. "You mean the costumes, right?"

"Yes," he said.

"I agree with you about that. Who would dress this way? Even for a good cause? I think my wife might be a librarian," I said pointing at her.

"HA!" he laughed, "She isn't a librarian. That is Mary Katherine Gallagher from Saturday Night Live skits."

"Oh, yeah. Hey, I feel better about that." I shook his hand, "I am Bob. I am guessing you were archery hunting?"

"Yep," he shook hands firmly and with some joy. "I am Steve. You a grouse hunter?"

"Nah," I said. "At least not most of the time. Rabbits. But I shoot some birds with the beagles."

"I love beagles. Haven't had one since I was a kid."

"Yeah? Well, grab some of those tiny burgers and we will go give them a treat." We were two rural minded guys in a world that has gone crazy, strolling towards my truck.

"Say," I asked, "do you have a maid or a gardener?"

"No!"

"Good," I sighed. We went to see the dogs and talk about the finer philosophical points of life—most notably autumn.

A Good Knife

We often think of spring as being the most difficult time on a child when it comes to concentrating on their schoolwork, especially as they near the end of the academic year and a brief work release is granted to students as they leave the educational penitentiary and gladly mow lawns, weed gardens, pick berries, and split firewood. This was back in the 1900s when they did not require national campaigns persuading kids to play for one hour each day. We rushed through several hours of chores and then relaxed with an afternoon of vigorous bicycle riding and baseball. Certainly the last weeks of the school year had me yearning for chores and fun.

October, however, was my hardcore daydreaming month. I don't know how people can possibly concentrate on work with the autumnal colors gradually flushing into the foliage; like the blush on an embarrassed person's face as he slowly realizes why he is embarrassed. Each autumn day brings colors more vibrant than the last. I could not refrain from looking outside, no matter how hard I tried. I have the same problem today, and there are thick drapes on the window of my office preventing me (if I use the drapes) from being totally overwhelmed by the excitement that fall necessarily brings with it.

When I was a kid, October was the time when I could not wait to go rabbit hunting again. By October, it had seemed like forever since I was allowed to shoot a rabbit. In reality, it had been since early January, or nearly forever in kid chronology. Oftentimes the daydreaming had to find a way to express itself. So, we boys would talk about hunting while standing near the window and waiting for the bell to ring for the next class.

"I'm going squirrel hunting this weekend," a kid would mention.

"Gray or fox squirrels?" another would interrogate in a matter of fact fashion, even if he had never seen a fox squirrel.

"My dad and I are hunting grouse," the conversation might shift focus. All of this would happen as other students filled the room and sneakers squeaked on the floors. The bell would ring, and we would sit and listen to our teachers talk about dangling modifiers or integers or historical dates. Meanwhile we would stare out the window and prepare our next conversations after the bell. Rabbit season opened after squirrel and grouse, so my angst intensified each week.

Naturally, we would produce the occasional pocket knife and rub our thumb across the blade, perpendicular to the edge, in order to test it for sharpness. Then we would hand it to our friends, offering them the handle, for them to test the blade as well. As I mentioned, this was in the 1900s, and a pocketknife was not at all uncommon. They were handy in shop classes and science labs alike. Our pocketknives were sharper than anything our biology teacher gave us for dissection. She never got mad.

"Be careful you boys don't puncture the entrails of your frog," she might say. At that point it was important to have a ready answer. "Don't you worry, ma'am; this knife has done some gutting!" was a good answer that demonstrated hunting prowess.

If a kid brought a pocketknife to school now they would be medicated for a mood disorder, given a time out, and then arrested as a threat to national security. Like I said, it was different then. My first pocketknife was a *Case*, and Dad taught me how to sharpen it with a whetstone. The important thing about a whetstone is that you have to sharpen both sides of the knife at the same angle and for the same amount of time or you are just wearing away the steel.

I had used my knife all summer, mostly at the newsstand. The new comic books came on Wednesday, and I would go downtown with my paper route money to by 5 comic books each week. That would cost exactly three dollars. It was three dollars and eighteen cents if they charged tax—they never really did come to a consensus on whether comic books ought to be taxed.

Anyway, the new comics and new magazines were in the back room waiting to be displayed, but I was allowed to go back and sort through the new comics before they went onto the rack. They were bound together in a plastic, yellow band that was stretched tight and held together with an adhesive stronger than any you can buy. So, I would use my trusty pocketknife to free the heroic, colorful narratives from their bindings. It took some effort, but with enough pressure, the bands would suddenly burst apart with a twang like a steel cable breaking.

There was also whittling, where I would turn limbs that were knocked down by storms into toothpicks. Sometimes, while letting the beagles chase rabbits I would find a larger limb and shave the bark before cutting away at the stick to make the perfect length for a walking stick. A good walking stick would last for years, or until you stumbled upon a stick that looked like it would work better than the one you were currently using. I usually changed walking sticks once per week. Minimum. Once I had liberated enough comic books and customized some walking sticks, the blade would need sharpened.

I found that I did not do a good job of keeping the angle the same as I used the whetstone. I would do my best and then put the knife away. By the time I had developed the knack for using the stone, I had ground away a lot of metal from the blade—maybe a third of it. Or more. So, when we were talking about the upcoming rabbit season and I produced my bunny blade, it was greeted with audible gasps.

"Holy cow," Joe said.

"Yeah, how about it? Nice, right?" I replied, trying to be nonchalant.

"What happened to this thing?" Bill winced.

"What do you mean?"

"It's like half the blade is missing," Bill marveled.

"Nah," I dismissed him, "that's just a well used knife with plenty of good steel for future hunts."

"Didn't you just get this thing last spring, for trout season?" Joe stared at the knife wide-eyed.

"I read a lot of comic books this summer," I said. I had also made a lot of walking sticks. I did, by the way, learn how to use the whetstone with all of the practice that summer provided.

I was thinking about all of these things recently while admiring a new *Case* knife that I have been using, and my wife, Renee, walked into the room.

"Don't cut yourself!" Renee yelled. I jumped when she yelled, almost cutting myself.

"Jeepers!" I yelled back. "I almost got hurt."

"Well, no wonder," she held her hands out to the side as if pointing out the obvious. "You are staring out the window and rubbing your thumb across that knife. You could get cut!"

"I wasn't going to get cut. You don't run your thumb in the same direction of the blade," I pointed out the obvious.

"What are you looking at?"

"That maple tree," I explained. "See how some yellow color is setting into the leaves?"

"Is that what you were thinking about?"

"Sorta," I closed the knife, "but I was also thinking about the beagles and how they are in good shape for the hunting season in a few weeks." I opened the blade and looked at it again. "Oh, and I was thinking about how glad I am that you have that knife sharpening kit for your kitchen knives. Do you mind if I use it sometimes?"

"That's fine," she closed the thick drapes in my office. "Now get to work."

GRAVY

Thanksgiving will be here before we know it, and I can't help but be amazed at what happened last year. You see, holidays are a stressful time for families, and there is a limit to how much time some people can tolerate their relatives. This seems like a very cynical thing to say, but it can often be true.

My Thanksgiving spread is more of a buffet, and it is designed for people to stop and then leave again. It is all wild game, and I like to think that the meal provides a brief respite from the tensions that can arise when relatives get together. I make it clear that my alternative Thanksgiving is meant to supplement, not replace your own Thanksgiving meal, unless you are alone that day and then you can come over for the duration. Most stop for a bit and leave.

"I am supposed to be getting batteries for the kids' video games," Lenny said last year as he ladled a bowl of rabbit stew from the parade of slow cookers that lined our kitchen counter, intended to keep food ready for our revolving door of guests. "But I am here because—and I never thought I would say this—I am sick of football."

"Did you hit your head?" I asked. "You love football."

"My brother-in-law is in town for dinner," Lenny extended his hands and spread the fingers further than I thought possible to show his angst. "He thinks he is a professional football gambler. He plays paper football for money and he has players in today's games."

"What is paper football?"

"Maybe it is called pretend football. They make fake teams using players from all the real teams. But on paper only."

"Oh, yeah," I said, "it's called fantasy football. I know some guys that research that stuff like it was a major scientific endeavor."

"That's my brother-in-law!" Lenny sputtered. "He buys magazines and statistics stuff and works on that stuff trying to make a bunch of money. He got upset about a dropped pass in the game today and went crazy and yelling cuss words. My wife sent me for batteries so I could cool off."

"Well, there's pheasant noodle soup here," I said, "and don't forget the sasafrass tea or the squirrel pot pie. The Buffalo dove dip is good too." We walked outside with light jackets and watched the beagles beg for a few bits of food. Soon we were greeted by Bill, who was temporarily avoiding the "debate" between his wife and her mother about potatoes.

"What kind of argument could taters possibly cause?" Lenny asked.

"It has to do with whether to use a masher or a mixer," Bill shrugged his shoulders, as if he wasn't quite sure if he properly understood the debate.

"Oh, yeah?" I was intrigued.

"My wife likes to use the handheld thing with the beaters. Her mom likes to use a masher. I thought I solved the argument by suggesting that they each make a batch, but it turns out we didn't have a hand masher anywhere. It got loud at that point . . ." his voice trailed off as he tried to reconcile his disbelief with the reality he actually witnessed.

"He needs some stew," Lenny went into the house to get him some. Before long we were reminiscing about rabbit hunts and sneaking a little bit of table scraps to the hounds. We laughed and thought about the fun of hunting. Bill's tale sounded familiar to me, as my mother and her mom could not share a kitchen very well either. I remember those childhood discussions well.

"Two hens can't cook one turkey," my dad would say as we departed for the briars every Thanksgiving morning to hunt rabbits. We didn't have a wild game dinner for the holiday when I was a kid, mostly because my gram was opposed to it, but also because Dad wasn't fond of arguing with my grandmother, who insisted on cooking a capon every year.

Mom always cooked a turkey, and she was always eligible for the biggest bird the store had due to her shopper's card loyalty points from the market. She was a savvy shopper and always bought the stuff that was on sale. Then she created menus for the week based upon what specials she found. Her Thanksgiving spread was huge. By the time Mom and Gram had their last argument about what temperature to set the oven and how long the massive turkey would have to cook before the capon was added to the bottom rack, my father and I would be listening to a rabbit chase.

"Remember," Dad said as he puffed his pipe, "it doesn't really matter how many rabbits we get."

"Should I shoot any?" I asked.

"You can," he sighed "but let's have a three circle rule. No rabbit gets shot until it has run three circles."

"Okay," I said, "but why is that? We usually have a one circle rule."

"We better stock up on good sounds now—like those beagles chasing rabbits. We may have missed most of the arguing, but there is gonna be a dispute at dessert time over whether they serve your mom's pumpkin pie or your gram's sweet potato pie. Those sounds won't be near as pleasant."

We sat in silence and listened to the hound music. I suppose that I have always found the song of the chase to be a welcome vacation from disharmony ever since. All the voices of a pack work together as they worry the rabbit through brush piles, push it around groves of trees, and drive it across the open fields. The hounds may compete but always with the same goal of pursuing the bunny. They hark to each other and readily recognize the times when their pack mates are doing well.

My wife, Renee, and I are already making preparations for the feast, altering the menu as the freezer accumulates wild game. My hounds have always flushed birds while they chase rabbits, and so the procession of crock pots has a changing course of dishes. I believe we are making biscuits this year, and turkey gravy to pour over them—if I get a turkey. Woodcocks are always wrapped in bacon and cooked on low heat over the grill. Trout are a frequent menu item, depending upon how many are left in the freezer from the summer.

Venison steaks are always popular, and I keep them sliced thin and chilling in a marinade, awaiting guests before I grill them. I keep the charcoal grill burning all day to whip up steaks whenever guests arrive. Some come early, some come late. A few have been known to make several visits.

The rabbit stew is always popular. Renee does most of the work, and even if the original recipes were mine, she has made them better. I always begin Thanksgiving the same way that I did as a kid—by taking the beagles to the field for a hunt with a three circle minimum per rabbit before I will shoot. I don't know why I still wait three circles, I suppose because it was what my father and I always did. There isn't really much conflict in my house, as my wife loves to putter around the kitchen, and I love to let her. But I know that the holidays can be terribly difficult for people that have family conflict. It can be even worse for the person who has no family in the immediate area. I try to not think of any of those things while the hounds and are hunting throughout the morning. I like their vocal melodies and rhythm to impose a harmony on the world, even if that harmony does not extend beyond the collective voice of the pack. For the time that we are afield, however, we enjoy the natural order in all of its perfection.

The food is ready at one o'clock in the afternoon, and I promise to be home by then. The dogs and I will then retreat to the yard, and I will sip the sassafras tea or hot cider while they circle the grill as I cook woodcock. They also pay too much attention to the smoker that is cooking the trout. The football games can be found on the television inside if you want to watch them. The dogs and I tend to receive visitors in the yard. All throughout the house are delicious foods; the main ingredients have been procured while I am in the briars and thickets listening to the hound song that soothes and calms all tensions in my life.

I like to think that the calmness of those hunts pervades the entire holiday. There is something delightful about the surprise of not knowing who is going to ring the doorbell next, although sometimes the guests will announce themselves as the dogs bark at the fence that obscures my sense of sight much more readily than it does their sense of smell. To be fair, not all of the guests are avoiding conflict or hiding from family. Many come to see what new recipes may have appeared this year. As we give thanks for all that we have, I am thankful for beagles and all the peace that they bring to my life. They certainly make life easier in a world that has headlines full of tragedy and family stories riddled with heartache. I hope the holidays can always be an occasion to extend a little joy to others. If you will excuse me, I still do not have that turkey for the end of the month, and I know a valley that normally has a flock in it. They run out of it every time the dogs chase a rabbit into the bottom, and I have been guessing wrong about their escape route every time I go there. I hope today is my lucky day—or it will be grouse gravy instead of turkey gravy over those biscuits.

Black Friday

Some of us are morning people. My wife, Renee, is not.
Typically, I am gone before she wakes up in the morning,
but there are times when the weather is foul and I am in
the kitchen whilst she undergoes her self-induced torture
which consists of waking up and slapping the snooze bar
every nine minutes; almost falling into deep sleep when the
contraption emits its aggravating, shrieking, monotonous
call again. On those rainy days when I am home for this
spectacle, I can hear her tromp across the room to renew
the snooze bar. She puts it across the room because it is
too easy to turn it off entirely if it is within arm's reach of
the bed.

She staggers downstairs and I offer her coffee. I have
learned that all communication is non verbal before she
has a chance to drink coffee. It took me a year to learn how
to translate the guttural sounds and lackadaisical hand
gestures that she uses instead of words before she has her
coffee. She is a night owl and often will work into the night
before watching television. I rarely am awake by the time
the eleven o'clock news begins. I tell you all of this to set
the stage for my favorite holiday—Thanksgiving.

I like to go hunting for the morning while my wife
cooks, and she likes to get up semi-early and start cooking
and watching a parade on television. I am in brush pants
at dawn, and she is in her pajamas until just a wee bit
before any company begins to arrive. We serve a wild game
dinner to an alternative crowd. By alternative crowd, I
mean people hiding from their families for a few minutes.
They can drop in anytime and sample from the five or six
wild game dishes that we have whipped up for the day.
There is no set time to eat, just stop by.

All the while she cooks, I am hunting rabbits. I look
forward to it all year, and I return in time to clean up and
put any new game from that day's hunt in the freezer. I

usually eat a lot of rabbit, pheasant, and venison, and ignore the desserts. I like to take pumpkin pie and nut roll as my snack food on the day after Thanksgiving when I go rabbit hunting again. The pie is always nice and cold after the overnight. I like it for breakfast with whipped cream and my morning coffee. The nut roll goes into my shirt pocket, wrapped snugly in plastic wrap, and is my lunch throughout the Friday hunt.

Last year I awoke and quietly snuck downstairs in the dark so that I did not disturb Renee. I walked into the hall and immediately smelled coffee. Much to my surprise Renee was awake and fully caffeinated. She set a cup of coffee down in front of me and said, "There ya go, hon," like she was a veteran waitress.

"What are you doing awake?" I said in absolute disbelief.

"I decided to get into this Black Friday Christmas shopping thing," she opened the refrigerator and cut a giant slab of pumpkin pie and then slid it across the table like it was a truck stop counter. "You want whipped cream, hon?" she asked.

I just sat there wondering what to think.

"Here's a warm up," she filled my coffee cup and walked away to get the whipped cream.

"Thanks," I said. "I will take some whipped cream. That's a big piece of pie."

"Well," she shook her head to the side to jog her memory, "I am usually asleep when you eat this stuff for breakfast, but I would say that is the size you eat, judging from the remains of the pie in the fridge when I wake up."

"Oh," I said, "well, I guess maybe I sometimes eat a piece and then cut another. So I usually eat two pieces, maybe."

"Okay Sweetie," she took a knife and cut my pie into two pieces and slid the whipped cream in front of me. Then she filled my coffee again, even though I hadn't drank much of it.

"Well, where are you going?" I asked.

"I am not sure." She held her hands on her hips. "You want your nut roll now too?"

"No, I take that in the woods with me," I said.

"What?"

"Can I get it to go?"

"You bet, hon." She put it in aluminum foil, which is not what I do, but I decided it was better for keeping the pastry from disintegrating in my shirt pocket.

"Well," I grabbed my coffee before she could fill it, "I will probably hunt until noon or later."

"No problem," she whisked away the plate that had previously held my pie. "Me and the girls won't be home until evening."

"Really?" I asked. "Can we afford that much shopping?"

"Yes, I am not buying stuff at every store. I am just going for the big sales."

"When do they happen?" I asked. "It is only five o'clock in the morning now."

"Oh," she slapped the nut roll down in front of me, "they are happening now. Some started last night."

"Last night?" I asked, "Did you go shopping last night?"

"Just for a couple hours while you and the beagles were sleeping on the couch after we ate."

"Wow, I had no idea."

"I was home and sitting in the living room when you woke up."

"I didn't hear your alarm clock." I thought out loud.

"I haven't been to sleep yet," she said. "I formulated a shopping plan that will let me be finished with all the Christmas shopping by the end of today. I was so amazed at the deals that I found last night I was inspired."

I put the tracking collars on the dogs and loaded them into the dog box. We kissed each other goodbye and went in our opposite directions. I decided to hunt until dark, as she had plans for an all day spree. It turns out that she enjoyed the outing, saved money, and was totally happy to let me rabbit hunt as late as I wanted. She slept right through the alarm the next day, and after I turned it off, I decided to go hunting. I can't prove it, but I am pretty sure she hadn't been awake very long when I came home with a limit of rabbits at eleven o'clock in the morning. I base that evaluation upon lackadaisical hand gestures and guttural sounds when I walked in the door.

SCHOOL BUS DRIVERS AND SANTA

While I can't prove it, I think that a criminal background check may be required for individuals applying for a job driving school buses in order to make sure that they have a criminal record. On many occasions in recent years, I have had the experience of being forced onto the shoulder of the road as a black and yellow school bus roars past me with the impression that the half of the road to which they were entitled was the middle half. No doubt this is because the bus driver can no longer yell, "You bleeping kids better knock that bleep off before I bleeping stop this thing and beat your bleeps!" That is what bus drivers once did, way back in the 1900s when I was a kid.

I would be very surprised if the drivers were allowed to even raise their voices when talking to children, and it is more likely that the drivers must attend some sort of sensitivity training where they can be taught how to make each and every child feel not only affirmed, but special. The kind of special that permits someone to have additional privileges and benefits. Certainly the pay is less than stellar, so there are bound to be some drivers lacking skills. For instance, when I am at the church office in the afternoon and the bus is letting kids go for homework release from school until the morning, the driver makes me move my truck.

First of all, I call it homework release because if you have ever had a kid in elementary school, then you will know how much more homework kids have now compared to the days of yore. It apparently isn't working, if you ever read the results of the standardized tests that the youngsters have to take, almost every year. Secondly, the reason that he makes me move my truck is because it is

often the only vehicle parked along the right curb as he drives down the street. The left hand side has all sorts of cars parked there, since it is a neighborhood with homes. Mind you, the town plow, cement trucks, fire engines, and trailers being towed to the local carnival have no difficulty fitting down the street with cars parked on both sides.

Another bus driver in our town once had to go all the way up a hill that dead ends at a cemetery. The last kid lived at the house of one of my parishioners. Fortunately for him, the kid's mother was home in the morning, because she had to direct him as he turned the bus around in her spacious driveway. Every day. He never did figured it out, and I suppose he was pleased as punch when the kid finally graduated.

I say all of this as an introduction to my own bus driver as a kid. I think, though my memory may be fuzzy, that her name was Joan. We kids had to gather at bus stops then, rather than the bus stopping every 20 feet like it does now. In theory the bus stop was designed to limit the number of times that the drivers had to let kids board in the morning and disembark in the afternoon, thereby making the drive shorter in time. This may have been true, but the bus stop also allowed kids to become accustomed to the reality of bullies and conflict.

As surprising as it may sound, kids walked to these bus stops and no parents were present. In my school grades k-6 got on the bus together. As you can imagine, there was a large difference in the size of the oldest kids and the youngest. For instance, when I was in first grade there was a 6th grader by the name of Bubba that was a bully who was shaving already. It was impressive, even when you considered the fact that he had flunked two years and should have been in eighth grade.

Anyway, Bubba was always at the bus stop early to intimidate other kids. It was sort of his main reason for actually attending school. The younger group of kids employed various strategies to avoid his taunting, pushing, punching, and bad breath. We sometimes tried showing up just before the bus arrived, but this risked the potentiality of missing the thing altogether, and that meant returning to the house and making mom take me. Better to take a beating from Bubba. We also would arrive in a group, using the herd mentality and relying on the fact that it would be a classmate on the outside of the group or the slowest kid to actually be caught by Bubba. I could usually outrun at least one other kid.

The bus was another matter, and Bubba would set up his extortion business at the back, where he would collect our lunch money for his personal use. One of the main strategies to defend against this side business that he had established was to sit directly behind the bus driver, Joan. I tried to wiggle my way into the front of the line. When the door of the bus opened, a wall of cigarette smoke billowed into the air. It was a spectacular sight in the winter. Joan had a beehive hair-do and an unfiltered cigarette bounced on her bottom lip the entire time she spoke. This may seem quite out of place by today's educational scene. The teacher's lounge, of course, was the same way and kids would periodically get a glimpse of a teacher emerging from the lounge with freshly mimeographed quizzes. It looked very much like the tests were being rescued from a towering inferno by a firefighter as the smoke flowed into the hallway. Mimeographs, by the way, are how copies were made before photocopiers for any of you youngsters that might be reading. If the copies were fresh the bluish ink would still be wet.

Joan would talk to you if you sat in the seat behind her, especially at stop signs where she would light a new cigarette and throw the butt of the finished one out the window. "What do you want for Christmas?" Joan asked me one day as she slip shifted the behemoth from the stop sign while lighting a smoke.

"I would like a dog," I said.

"Santa isn't always good about dogs," she jammed the diesel into a higher gear and flicked ash out the window.

"Oh," I said, "I didn't know that."

"Yeah," she said, "puppies get cold in Santa's sleigh."

"Well, I know a kid that got one last year."

"He can haul a few puppies," she said, "at his feet."

Joan sure knew what she was talking about. Santa didn't bring me a dog. And I asked for one every year after that. When I was in sixth grade, several kids I knew had beagles that were chasing rabbits and so did my relatives. I was thoroughly enthused and could not wait to get one. Then, when I was twelve years old, I went rabbit hunting with a beagle. I was almost thirteen actually, as my birthday is in February and you could not hunt until you were twelve. My twelfth birthday was a bitter sweet affair—I was old enough to hunt, but small game and deer season had recently ended.

I had a paper route by that time, and I decided that I wanted to get serious about beagles. My paper route money was good income, and Christmas time was the bonanza of tips. Some customers gave twenty dollars as a tip for the holiday. I bought my first rabbit shotgun with a wad of five dollar bills, the most common Christmas tip for my paper route. The same was true for my first beagle the following summer. I was lucky; my first beagle was a good hunting dog, and I was able to shoot a lot of rabbits over him.

There are plenty of people that hunt rabbits, but from the first time I hear a hound sing the song of the chase I was hooked as a houndsman. It's a lifestyle, really, much more than just a hobby. As Christmas nears, I can't help but think of all the puppies that Santa will give and the subsequent trip that many dogs will make to the shelter as people discover that their cute puppy has grown into a barking and howling dog. But you know what else I have thought about? The great joy that comes when a kid becomes hooked on hounds. I suspect that Santa will be leaving video games and other electronics at lots of houses this year. I wonder how much better our sport would be if we made sure that youngsters interested in rabbit hunting got a good beagle.

PICTURE THIS

Well, it has happened again. Christmas has gone crazy again. First it was cookies. My wife was really involved with Christmas cookies, and it was fancy cookies with exotic ingredients that she and her friends would exchange. Then she decided to get very involved in making homemade Christmas cards. When I say very involved, I mean a room full of ribbons, pretty paper, cardboard stock, paints, glitter (oh, the glitter), paint, machines for cutting designs, festive ink stamps, and all sorts of other things that required trips to places that sell storage bins. The Christmas cards took more time to construct than I could have possibly imaged. The process of making these cards culminated in a late night frenzy wherein I awoke to find her covered in glue and glitter with a pile of cards ready to be mailed. That was December 22.

Anyway, this year the obsession is a Christmas photo that we can mail to our friends. The original plan was to have a picture of our family with the beagles sitting politely. The beagles, of course, are not cooperating with this plan. By some odd coincidence, I managed to place a couple dogs in a few trials last year, and they would not cooperate when it came time to pose on the bench. The Christmas photo went even worse, so we have moved on to a back-up plan wherein we just let the dogs do what they want and hope that the picture comes out okay.

Christmas presents are a real challenge anymore. I would like to see everyone get a GPS collar for every dog, but that is a rather expensive. I always find myself stuck while trying to find a gift idea for my beagle friends. In my defense, I never do well at buying gifts for people. The main problem is that I never know what to get my wife. I have a good solution to this, however. I ask a married woman that is close to the same age what she wants for Christmas. Very often this causes some confusion, as the lady presumes I am buying her a present. I explain that I just want to know what she wants so I can buy the same thing for my wife, and I will be thankful enough that I will tell her husband what to get her. This works relatively well, although it has flopped a couple times.

Once, I got those knee high boots (with no arch support) that are commonly worn by women in the winter. It turns out that my wife, Renee, doesn't like those. On another occasion I purchased a purse that was popular at the time, and it was a failure as well. Oh well, I try. Frequently, however, this strategy works quite well, and it can save a lot of time in guessing. My other strategy, of course, is to go to the stores on Christmas Eve and choose from whatever happens to be left on the shelves. The lack of options is comforting to me, in ways that are hard to explain. I guess the appeal is in not having too many choices. My favorite restaurant for breakfast, Green Acres (I presume it is named after the television show) has a sign on the door that says they do not accept credit cards. The register has a sign that informs the patron that they do not accept checks. We all go there with cash. A lack of choice is liberating in ways that the psyche understands. Of course, there is also a liberation that takes place when my wife opens her gift to reveal car seat covers for Christmas—she liberates her emotions from being remotely pleased with the fact that I have solved the problem of dog hair on the seats of her car.

"You bought me car seat covers."

"Yeah, obviously."

"I thought you were just using this box that says 'car seat covers' to avoid wrapping the gift. I didn't know you got me car seats."

"The stores were out of wrapping paper."

"They don't run out. You weren't looking in the right place."

"Well, I know you hate dog hair on your back when you go to work so I got these."

"That was kinda sweet. But not romantic." That happened several Christmases ago, and a bad situation was avoided.

I am now bad about shopping in stores and have decided that all gifts must come from the internet, or I am not buying them. And that has got me thinking about gifts for my beagling friends. All the hunts we share, and the laughs at field trials. We help each other out, and we share one another's pain at the loss of our beloved canine hunting partners.

So I found a way to say Merry Christmas to all my beagle friends—I make the gift on the computer and reinstate the homemade card fiasco. Somewhere, in the bowels of the camera roll on my phone, I have pictures of my friends after a rabbit hunt, or hanging out at the club and conditioning dogs. I have pictures of my buddies posing beagles on the bench after they have won a ribbon. Yep, I have decided not to send you a picture of my family, but rather one of you in a happy time that we shared afield. Maybe I will send you some homemade cookies too. Merry Christmas, my friends.

Wool Socks and Fresh Bread

As a kid I was never a fan of clothes for Christmas gifts. This is because kids are not too smart about needs versus wants. My grandmother was one of those women who had gnarled and twisted hands from knitting, quilting, sewing and various other activities that required needles, thread, yarn, and fabric. By the time I was a teenager, I had learned that my best presents were wool socks. This was in the old days, before Goretex and similar materials were in existence. If they did exist they were not affordable. The primary sock to keep dry feet was bread bags.

Bread bags were a little difficult to come by in the winter. This is because my mother only bought sliced bread in the summer. Once it was cold enough to bake, she would make the bread. This was especially good in the fall, because the baking would warm the house. The alternative was to have dad build a fire in the wood burner that was in the basement.

My father was a jack-of-all-trades kind of guy. He was a fantastic carpenter, but he could also do residential electric work, cement, and plumbing. Plumbing was his least favorite, and I often learned bad words when he was doing plumbing work. I would see my friends when I was a little kid and impress them with a new vulgarity that Dad had muttered under his breath while soldering. Many of the words we would not even be able to define until high school. I think this is why my mother preferred that I not accompany my father when he would go fix plumbing for neighbors and relatives. I was his chief gopher.

Anyway, he hooked up the wood stove to a ductwork system that utilized a fan to blow the hot air into the rooms of the house. There was a thermostat of some sort that would force the air through the ductwork and into the two floors above the basement. It would engage when the internal temperature of the furnace reached a sufficiently hot temperature. It basically ran non-stop in the winter, and the blower would keep the stove from reaching meltdown temperatures. The only reason we never had a chimney fire was that Dad had some chemical that was tossed into the fireplace on the top of burning coals that cleaned the lining in the chimney and caused the dust to fall to the cleanout door. It is probably not a legal chemical now but was commonly sold then and would flare up like a fireball when a scoop of the powder was pitched onto the blue-hot coals. The thermostat on the wall in our living room was once connected to a natural gas stove. This was in the 1970s when methane was very expensive and dad disconnected that furnace. The wall thermostat only had one function—to serve as a thermometer to tell us how hot it was in the house.

"94 degrees," I once said looking at that thermometer. "I think I will go outside and shovel the sidewalk."

"You did," Mom replied, "this morning."

"I know. I am going to cover the sidewalk again so dad will send me back out to clean it again later tonight. That will give me two breaks from the heat."

Dante wrote his famous work about the 9 levels of hell. Our house had three. The upstairs only had one heat vent. When the fire was really roaring you could sleep in your underwear and a light bed sheet all winter. There were times when it was hotter sleeping in January than during the humid nights of August in my bedroom. Even so, it was better than the ground floor which had a couple heat vents. Our downstairs had three rooms lined up in a row like a shotgun shack. The windows were open a lot in the winter.

The basement was the place you could find my father stoking the furnace as if we were about to forge steel. He would heave, it seemed, a cord of wood at a time into the fire, and smile with satisfaction as the house warmed. He was forever outside in the winter fixing porch steps, banisters, roofs, and whatever other side work he could get. The basement was full of firewood including a pile of kindling. The kindling would've been entirely unnecessary if Dad didn't have to go to work. We would let the fire burn to ash when he was working. This was in the days before 24-hour cable stations and newspapers were popular. Dad read 5 different papers each day, and a stack of them was always available for him to kindle a new fire. I once heard a forester describe the roar of a forest fire, and I think I can almost imagine it, based upon the sound of the furnace of my youth. Where was I?

Yes, Mom baked bread. She did this, I think, so that Dad would not have an excuse to start a wood fire. She would bake desserts for us and the aged neighbors. Supper was often a roast or some other long cooking meal. No bread bags. In hunting season I would often beg for bread bags from the neighbors for my own hunting boots. The only problem with bread bags was that feet would sweat and get a little wet but not as wet they might get from walking in muck, mud, snow, and water. It was during the great bread bag shortage of 1986 that I discovered my gram's wool socks did not require a bag over top of them. Her wool socks were warm and dry, and all I had to do was make sure that I limited the moisture intake to snow and did not step in water. Wool socks were my favorite gift after that. She also made woolen sweaters I never wore to school because they did not look fashionable.

For the record, I do not really understand fashion, and I have been accused of being pathetically utilitarian about my wardrobe, but at the time I was very interested in getting a girlfriend, and I felt that the sweaters would prevent me from having any dating success. Looking back, I have to rethink my logic at the time, since I did not have any dating success without the sweaters either. I took the wool sweaters out of my dresser drawers and placed them into the large duffle bag that held my hunting clothes. They were perfect for hunting, and I think may have rivaled the clothing that Woolrich, a company from my home state of Pennsylvania, was making at the time.

The second rabbit season is after Christmas in my home state as well, and I look forward to wool! I wear it all the time, actually, because I do not have to be worried about fashion since I am married. This is one of the greatest benefits of marriage. My wife is actually allergic to wool so she won't hug or lean on me while I am wearing it. Even so, it is great for warding off the chill. My wife and I are a little more conservative with our thermostat, preferring to be economical, and long sleeves and sweaters are commonly worn in our home. My dad had free firewood and free labor to split and stack it. I was the free labor. My home has a wood pellet stove, which takes most of the labor out of burning wood while simultaneously adding a lot of expense. I miss free heat.

I miss my gram's socks more. I am sure the ones I have now are just fine. I am sure they are as warm. Store bought does not make them bad. But I miss seeing her sit in the rocker and make them as fast as can be, and I miss the warmth from Mom's kitchen oven as she turned out pies and cookies with the loaves of bread in order to keep the house warm enough that my father didn't go to the basement and engage the blast furnace. I have moved many times (for school and work) since I last received Gram's socks and sweaters. I don't have any left, not one.

There is something about winter that makes me love to come home. The inviting glow of yellow light from the windows in the pitch black night, the odors of slow cooked food, the sound of plows scraping the road on a day when school is cancelled and everyone stays home. I am thinking about sweaters and socks, and the powerful memories that they invoke—the perfect gift that meets needs and not wants. Indeed, memories of wool allow me to invoke the sentiments of love from the past when my parents and grandmother were still living. Christmas is coming. My thoughts are going to be focused on a desire to hunt bunnies, hopefully in a place that allows me to wear snowshoes as I tromp through pines and hemlocks.

I even have thoughts of the impending snowshoe hare season. It is short here, and there are not many, but I grew up in the hottest spot in the state to find them. I have treasured memories of my father and I going afield to hunt them in the second shopping season. The second shopping season was when my mom and sister would go to the stores to take advantage of deals that the stores would make to unload the merchandise that was not sold in the glut of commercialism that preceded Christmas day.

The last time I hunted with Dad was a hare hunt during Christmas break while I was a freshman in college. He was dying of cancer, but at the time he thought the problem was that his back was arthritic from all the years of hard labor. He had been cancer free for years, and his last checkup revealed nothing. We both shot hare and cottontail that day. We almost didn't go since I was more interested in hanging out with friends that I had not seen since summer and his back hurt badly. I decided I would hunt and hang out with my friends at night, and my father went along. That was the last time I saw him well enough to hunt. He loved hound music, so we were in no hurry to shoot hare. We just drank coffee on the tailgate for the first hour of the first chase.

These are the memories that swarm my mind about Christmas. I forget all the toys I ever coveted for the holiday. Baked bread, hunts, and socks. That's it. By the time I ended my second semester of college dad was bedridden, and he was gone before I started my third semester. I think he knew something was wrong—he installed a high efficiency gas furnace after I moved to college and reconnected the thermostat on the wall. The Christ child came to save us, and if we are careful we can celebrate the holidays even without our loved ones that have gone before us. They live forever because of the birth proclaimed by a star.

I have a pair of wool socks made by a parishioner. I am going to make a sandwich with homemade bread for lunch and go hare hunting after Christmas. When the sound echoes just right in the Allegheny National Forest, I can hear dogs that have been dead for decades. I can smell the strong coffee that Dad makes. I may even shoot a hare, but only after listening to a long chase over coffee. I might even call my wife on the way home to have her set the thermostat real high so it feels like a real homecoming. Merry Christmas, and may your memories of happy times overwhelm you this season.

BEACH BUNNIES

Now that we are into the throes of winter, it could be that we are having a desire for warmer temperatures and summer scenery. What is more summery than the beach? My wife, Renee, is fond of the beach. Myself, I am not a beach guy. In part it is because I am a little pale. When I was a child, my hair was almost white, and it got darker as I aged. My beard once had some streaks of red in it, and it has since developed some blonde hair. Or grey, as my wife calls blonde. She may be color blind, I think. All of this means that I have a multi-stage process of tanning wherein I turn lobster red, and then my skin peels away. Then I will burn again before the skin will tan. Well, okay, it doesn't tan so much as it becomes a less translucent shade of white.

I also am not a beach fan because I encountered a jellyfish at the beach as a kid. I never saw the darn thing until it was too late, but I would rank the event with any wasp nest or ground hornets encounter I have experienced. I ran out of the water screaming as a kid, and things got worse from there when I fell onto the sand. I couldn't care less to go to the beach and fight the crowds of vacationers. I would prefer a trip into the mountains to escape the heat in the summer. I have taken my wife to the Adirondacks for vacation to chase hare with the beagles and her big job is to stay between the dogs and the one paved road that we worry about for dogs. We use walkie-talkies and she gets pretty bored, I am sure.

Renee constantly wants to go to a beach, and she always wants to drag me with her. A few years ago we were at a conference in McAllen, Texas. If you have never been there, you can save yourself the trip by going to bed at night and listening to recordings of police sirens and ambulance whistles all night long from the convenience of your own home. The conference center would not let us go anywhere alone, preferring to give all guests free rides to any destination and back again. "We don't want you getting robbed," the shuttle driver said.

At the end of the conference, we rented a car and drove out to South Padre Island. Sand dunes, warm water, and salt air refreshed my wife beyond words. I packed only boots and pants for the trip. I never wear shorts, since my legs can be dazzlingly white at times. I was sweating and the humidity was miserable as my wife removed her flip flops and waded into the ocean for her beach reward after a long conference. Most summers, however, Renee has to go to the beach with her aunt or friends. I may be persuaded to go to the beach more often, however, after my last trip.

Jason Wiseman invited me to go hunt cottontails on Cape Cod before I ventured north to Maine for some hare hunting. I quickly consulted my navigational system to see what options I had to get there. By navigational system, I mean an atlas. Don't get me wrong; I have a smarty pants phone that will tell me how to get to a location, but I like to memorize my route before I begin. It isn't entirely out of the ordinary for the smarty pants phone to be unaware of certain things like road construction either. Needless to say, all the routes from my house to Cape Cod looked like they passed through heavily congested areas. While on the phone I asked Jason, "How bad is the traffic in Connecticut?"

Now, I am the field trial secretary at two different beagle clubs, one of which is West Branch Beagle Club. Our club has hills. Now that I think about it, there is nothing flat on the whole running grounds. The hills are steep enough that going down may be worse than going up. I have seen judges tumble to the bottom. In addition to the main hills, there are various "hollows" or "gullies" or "depressions" that mandate further climbs and descents. When a potential new judge asks me about the hills my response is always the same: "There is some slope because it's Pennsylvania. It ain't that bad though." This, of course, is a lie. We should have mules on hand for our judges. Remember I mentioned that I asked Jason about the traffic in Connecticut?

"There is some traffic because it is Connecticut," Jason replied. "It ain't that bad though." I should have known then that he was not being truthful. He was using the same technique I do when getting judges. Hartford, Connecticut is 5 lanes wide, and no one is in the lane that they want. It rained the whole drive. My rural inclinations had to go into full blown hillbilly mode to drive through that mess. I white-knuckled the steering wheel until the Massachusetts border! I am now going to be more honest with potential judges at our club and tell them, "By the time you get to the bottom to see the pack the beagles will be almost back to the top. And you can't run those hills as fast as the dogs. Also, there is a creek and swamp in the bottom. Oh, and it is very slippery running downhill. You may want to bring extra socks from sweating and extra pants and shirts from slipping on the mud. Now what class did you say you would judge?"

Even with the hills it is worth coming to our club, just as Cape Cod was worth the traffic. Granted, I was there in late October, after the tourist season, but I had a blast. There are a lot of beaches there, and I called my wife when I arrived at my friend's house.

"I am here," I said.

"Okay, what is going on?" She asked.

"Just supper tonight, and then tomorrow we are going to go looking for beach bunnies!" I said. Now that is not a statement that many men have made to their wives. That is because my wife knew that I was talking about rabbits that ran along the beach. I should tell you that I had some reservations about these beach bunnies. When I think about scenting conditions, I would say that dry, wind-swept sand sounds about as bad as it gets for a hound. I say that having run dogs on dirt roads, crusty snow, shale stone at the edge of a coal mine, and even a gravel road.

Jason had dogs accustomed to the sand, and my dogs figured it out faster than I thought they would. I have dogs that use their eyes though, and they will look for rabbit tracks in the snow. They quickly realized that they could see the little footprints of the bunnies in the sand dunes! I could not have been more pleased with the whole experience. I never imagined hunting for rabbits on a beach. Of course there are brushy areas near the beach, which is where the rabbits eat and live. It is something special to watch a cottontail run into the sand in an attempt to lose the dogs on the poor scent. My biggest worry was the dogs drinking salt water before I could give them the bottled water I carried with me.

Also, my three hounds looked like a million bucks when they got to Maine. It was an easy transition for my dogs to go from running cottontails on the sand dunes of Cape Cod to chasing snowshoe hare in the swamps of Maine. I talked to my wife as I drove to Maine.

"So, did you bag any beach bunnies?" she asked.

"Oh yeah," I said, "I had a great time."

"Well, good, I am glad."

"I think you should go to the beach with me next time."

"Next time? You are going back to the beach?"

"Yes, I am. You could enjoy the shoreline while I hunt."

"I might be able to do that," she sounded cheery.

"We will bring the walkie-talkies. If the dogs run to drink the ocean water you will have to intercept them for me." I think I heard her roll her eyes over the phone.

Bird Brain

I have a dog named Duke, and his sire, Rebel, liked
birds. There was a bird feeder in my yard when Duke was a
pup, and he smelled bird scent all over the yard. He would
also go out into the yard and graze on seed that had spilled
out of the feeder. Duke loves birds even more than Rebel
did. All birds. Even a sparrow, or robin, or chickadee, or
blue jay. In the early small game season, I have had hunts
where he would bag doves, woodcock, grouse, and
pheasant and we would never shoot a rabbit. In part this
was because he will pursue bird scent when he finds it, at
least until he encounters rabbit scent, but there is also the
consideration that he I have many hunting spots where the
rabbits can run within a few yards of me, and I do not see
them due to the density of the overgrowth. I shoot way
more rabbits after the frost and snow knock down some of
the vegetation.

When he goes onto these bird diversions, I call him
Winslow—it sounds more fancy and expensive. Like a
setter or some other gentlemanly breed. I also call him
bird-brain when he is flushing sparrows, cowbirds, and
other avian diversions that are not game species. I could
always tell when he was chasing birds, because he actually
clucked like a chicken instead of baying like a hound. He
sounded like a chicken when he was chasing birds. And he
did it slowly. Until recently.

At the end of the previous hunting season, Duke
caught a pheasant and retrieved it to me. Don't think
about wild pheasant like in the mid-west, but rather think
large, free-ranged chickens. The game commission stocks
them here in Pennsylvania, and they have a certain cult
following. The stocking schedule is printed in the
newspapers, and it is rather like in the spring when they
stock trout in streams. There are people that look for these
mostly tame critters.

Incidentally, I was watching them feed farm raised trout, and the food looked and smelled a little like the Purina Brand Moist & Meaty dog food—it is soft kibbles that come in plastic pouches. It works great for the stocked trout, who have spent most of their lives in the equivalent of a large fish tank waiting to be fed. I am not sure how long they must be in the wild to learn how to catch a minnow, but the dog food works great for catching them and getting a kid interested in fishing.

This brings me to the point of it all: those tame fish are good for introducing kids to the sport, but I have seen grown men knock kids out of the way to catch a trout that has only been in a river a few hours. The stocked pheasant are about the same. When they are newly released from the truck, they are pretty shocked. They will stand around and look at you. It is a fine opportunity to introduce kids to hunting, and they are way easier to hit than grouse. Often, however, I see hunters that are in the woods, without a dog, looking for a bird as wild as a chicken, and they are eager to kill. That is fine, I shoot the stocked birds too, but it becomes unsafe when they are shooting at moving brush because that is how they have had success—shooting the birds as they stand in the ground.

This is the whole reason that I put bells on my dogs, to protect them from the guys that are shooting at moving brush. A beagle looking for a rabbit is similar in appearance to a bird running through the same goldenrod. I shudder to think how I might react if someone shot my dog. Anyway, Duke caught a stocked pheasant last year, and I presumed it was wounded. I went to ring its neck and it flew as fast as can be, directly into my face, knocked my hat off my head, and fluttered into the distance. Duke had caught a perfectly healthy, though not so smart, pheasant that had been farm raised and had almost none of its natural instincts to survive.

From that day forward he has been different. He no longer clucks like a chicken on a pheasant. He runs down the trail in full cry, sounding like he is chasing a rabbit and at the same speed as he would chase a rabbit. I was taken aback the first time this happened. I saw him on a sprint and giving voice so I looked for a place to wait for the bunny when a ring neck flushed about 100 yards in front of me. It happened again. So, I started running after him to get a shot at these not-so-bright birds as they flushed. Well, those birds made me look even dimmer than them, as I would be completely out of breath after running a 100 yard wind sprint in order to be within shooting range when the feathered beast decides to take flight.

I look even more stupider (see, my grammar is failing) when I was chasing after him and hurdling over downed logs and brush, trying to be close and it turned out that he was chasing a rabbit. It would take me a quarter of a mile to figure this out however, as the stocked birds would sometimes go pretty far before they flushed. The GPS collar tracks my distance too, and I was really logging some serious miles to shoot a few of the birds that were making me look bird brained.

Then, I had two incidents where guys without dogs shot a rabbit my Duke was chasing. One time it was on a sight chase at a distance that was way too close for comfort. I started reading the stocking schedule for pheasants so that I could avoid those sorts of hunters. The effect, however, was that Duke really likes birds now. I have become the best grouse & woodcock hunter you have ever seen. Except I miss them all. But boy do I have a dog that can get after them.

The peculiar thing is that he throws his head in the air and flips his ears back to smell the birds in the wind. Then he circles around until he locates them if they are sitting after a fight. If he comes across their scent trail where they have been walking, he just chases them like a rabbit until they fly. I often take a whole pack of beagles to the woods on Saturdays, but during the week I only get to hunt a couple hours each day. I have to take a dog that can sit quietly in the dog box while I do hospital and nursing home visits. Duke is the dog for this task. And he has helped bag some poultry this year.

Last November he threw his head back and walked into the thickets. I watched him run into some thick cover and then I heard an eruption of baying and bawling from the dog. He ran out and then started coming back. I realized it had to be a rabbit and prepared for the shot. Then a turkey come out on a galloping-strut and looked to be preparing to fly. I always say that turkey takeoff the same way that ducks land—giving the impression that they have never done it before. Awkward would be a compliment. Clumsy would be giving them too much credit. I could see the young Jake starting to flap. Duke's baying was 70 yards behind the bird, but he was gaining. Two shots from the 16 gauge, and the bird tumbled. It scurried into the tall grass, and I feared that I had lost it. A bit later Duke arrived, stuck his nose into a clump of grass I had stepped upon twice, and dragged the lifeless bird to me by the wing. Several years ago the law changed in Pennsylvania to allow the use of dogs for hunting turkey during the fall season, and I am glad that they did. It has really made a big difference.

The only problem I have now is that as much scent as pheasant must leave, turkey are even smellier, it would seem, to a dog. He will throw his head back and launch out into a mowed hayfield. I look out and see a flock of turkey running at the edge, often 400 yards away. I hate to use a training collar to break him from this habit, because I am allowed to shoot one turkey per year with him. The pheasant and grouse are a nice bonus too. So I am living with this bird brain distraction. I can run a pretty quick mile these days though.

EPIPHANY

The New Year is here! One of the things that I look forward to every January is the holiday of Epiphany. Epiphany has been celebrated in the Church longer than Christmas. I could probably ramble on about its roots, calendars, and differences in the holiday in the Eastern and Western churches. The word, in Greek, literally means "Shine upon" and it is a day that is celebrated for Christ being revealed to the broader gentile world, as evidenced by the magi coming to worship him. It is not Christmas, but it can be called the twelfth day of Christmas, if you start counting on the 26th. It is January 6th. Clear? Me neither.

Anyway, the important thing is that the day is NOT Christmas. I love Christmas, but my wife and I are both pastors, and that can make for a very hectic holiday. There is all the worry about Christmas pageants—needless worry really, as the kids will do a wonderful job, and if a child makes a mistake (or more likely, just sort of stops participating and gets distracted for small segments of time) it will often be a cherished memory by everyone except the kid's own parents.

Candles for the singing of Silent Night are another thing that can get people excited. That page of the hymnal is totally covered in wax from being read by candle light for so many years, and there is always someone that takes time after the service to remove wax from pew pads, carpet, and my robe. I get wax on my robe every year. I did the same thing with mustard on my clothes every time I ate a sandwich as a little kid. Okay, I still spill mustard sometimes. Please understand, I love Christmas, but it is a work day around here, albeit a very fun work day.

Epiphany gets way less attention. No one starts shopping on Thanksgiving for Epiphany. The crèche or manger is more central to the day than the Christmas tree. It is a great day to have a relaxed, family-oriented celebration of the Christ Child. I do so with a wild game dinner—usually venison and rabbit. The week after Christmas roughly corresponds to the very limited snowshoe hare season in Pennsylvania. The northern tier of the state holds some thriving pockets of the white ghosts, and I always enjoy hunting them. As a kid we were allowed to shoot 2 per day, but in recent years the population has sufficiently diminished that the daily limit is 1. I haven't shot many hare in my home state in years. Sometimes this is because the snow isn't present, and it just seems wrong to shoot one of the majestic, white symbols of big woods and wilderness while they are momentarily standing still on brown ground, sneaking in front of the baying dogs. Other years I have refused to shoot them because there are so few. I always chase them though.

There is something about the snow covered hemlock branches and the seemingly endless expanse of mountain laurel that opens my spirit to all of the truths that Christmas represents. I was born and raised in the Allegheny National Forest, so it always seems like a home coming to make the drive for an annual hare hunting pilgrimage. If the snow cooperates and I find a sizeable population, I will use a muzzleloader this year—a 16 gauge side by side percussion cap.

There was a time when I would go there in the summer to get the dogs transformed into solid muscle by letting them run a summer hare at night. The arrival of the eastern coyote has ended that practice, as they now own the night and I will not have dogs on the ground at dusk anymore. Those summers of my youth provided great chases and enabled me to scout for the short hunting season. When it comes to hunting the white ghosts of the big woods I am much more likely to go to New York and hunt them along the Canadian border. More recently I chased them in Maine. My first memories of snowshoe chases are at home, at the southern limit of their range.

Epiphany is a favorite feast day. The season of Christmastide provides a great opportunity to get a few bunnies in the freezer for the big day. We invite a few friends and celebrate the light of the world. Speaking of light, there are a few tips I have for my fellow beaglers. One is for cleaning rabbits after a hunt that gets you home at dark. They sell battery powered, LED lights at any big box hardware store that are designed for cabinets. I attach velcro to several of these lights so that they can attach to my truck at the end of the day. I can then clean rabbits on the tailgate by taking the cabinet lights out of the glove box and sticking them up in the truck bed. They are great on the inside of your cap, on the side of the bed, or on a ladder rack or whatever you have above the tailgate.

A headlamp is another handy item to keep in a coat or vest for the arrival of darkness. When I was a kid a good headlamp was so heavy that it was the preferred means to build neck muscles for football players. The accompanying power source affixed to your belt and weighed slightly more than a battery from a large Buick. Since beaglers are not in the woods as late as coon hunters, we never carried much for a light, since we generally did not need one and it did not seem worth the extra weight. Now the lights are brighter and lighter than ever. I keep one just in case, and smetimes it is needed.

The nights are long and the days are short right now. It is in the winter that parking in my driveway causes me to pause and celebrate the golden light that pours from the house windows. Inside I know that supper is nearly ready. While summer finds me ready to eat supper quickly and take dogs to the beagle club, winter makes me content to eat and settle in front of the fireplace with the dogs. January 6th I will probably hunt a few cottontails in the valleys someplace and then return home for a day with family and feast that honors the gift of the Christ Child.

CPSIA information can be obtained
at www.ICGtesting.com
Printed in the USA
LVHW110305291220
675317LV00019B/250